D0187275

"The book of Proverbs is a gold mine of divine w[...]
applies that wisdom in very practical ways to the is[...]
of those books that should be studied more than simply read, and I can see it as a
valuable resource for women's Bible studies."

Jerry Bridges, author, *The Pursuit of Holiness*

"If only we could pull up a chair across from the purple-linen-wearing Proverbs 31
woman to observe her inner strength, listen to her confident laughter, admire her
reverent fear, and absorb her wise ways. That's what readers get to do through the
pages of *A Woman's Wisdom* as we're invited to saturate ourselves in the source
of true wisdom—the Scriptures—where we find what we need for living in a world
full of distractions, decisions, dilemmas, disappointments, and delights. This book
lends itself to quiet mornings of reflection on your own as well as vigorous discussions with a group of good friends."

Nancy Guthrie, Bible Teacher; author, Seeing Jesus in the Old Testament
Bible Study series

"It is so refreshing to read a book that handles the kinds of things that every
woman will face from one single perspective: the stunning wisdom of God. Too
often books like this start with cultural assumptions that only serve to weaken
their effectiveness in the end. It is only God's wisdom that can help us navigate the
pressures and insanities of the surrounding culture and teach us the freedom of
being what we were created to be and living as we were created to live. Read and
experience how God's wisdom is eloquent and transcendent while being concrete
and practical at the same time."

Paul David Tripp, President, Paul Tripp Ministries; author, *What Did You
Expect? Redeeming the Realities of Marriage*

"In a day when we're often inclined to settle for helpful hints or pious platitudes,
this book points us to the source of that rare commodity, true wisdom. Lydia
Brownback has the depth of insight and the lightness of touch needed to make the
book of Proverbs come alive for her readers. If your heart yearns for a solid place
to stand in the shifting currents of your everyday life, you will find a sure guide and
refreshing stream of truth here."

Liam Goligher, Senior Minister, Tenth Presbyterian Church, Philadelphia,
Pennsylvania; author, *The Jesus Gospel*

"Lydia Brownback has provided women with an excellent resource for unlocking
the wisdom of Proverbs."

Josh Moody, Senior Pastor, College Church, Wheaton, Illinois;
author *No Other Gospel*

"Halfway through the first chapter, I thought, 'My wife would love this book.' Halfway through the book, I thought, 'I love this book!' My reasons are manifold: Lydia Brownback's study of Proverbs is biblical, practical, straight-forward, convicting, instructive, transformative, and Christ-centered. With wisdom, wit, and carefully crafted sentences, Lydia Brownback's study of Proverbs helps women (and men!) to rest in the source of all wisdom, Jesus. See if you might 'love' the book as well."

Doug O'Donnell, Senior Pastor, New Covenant Church, Naperville, Illinois; author of *The Beginning and End of Wisdom*

"The beauty of proverbs is that, by their very nature, they are timeless and ageless. The smallest child can memorize and apply them on a surface level while the oldest adult can meditate on them and apply them over a lifetime. In this wonderful book, Lydia Brownback applies the proverbs to today's Christian woman. With equal parts sound interpretation and heartfelt application, this book offers that same timeless, ageless wisdom to a new generation of women."

Tim & Aileen Challies, Grace Fellowship Church, Toronto, Ontario; Tim blogs at Challies.com

"From the wisdom of Proverbs, Lydia Brownback draws wise and ever so practical applications for women. Her clear and consistent call is to embrace the full wisdom of God given to us in Christ."

Kathleen Nielson, Director of Women's Initiatives, The Gospel Coalition; author and speaker, Living Word Bible studies and *Bible Study: Following the Ways of the Word*

a woman's
WISDOM

Other Crossway books by Lydia Brownback:

Trust: A Godly Woman's Adornment

Contentment: A Godly Woman's Adornment

Purity: A Godly Woman's Adornment

Joy: A Godly Woman's Adornment

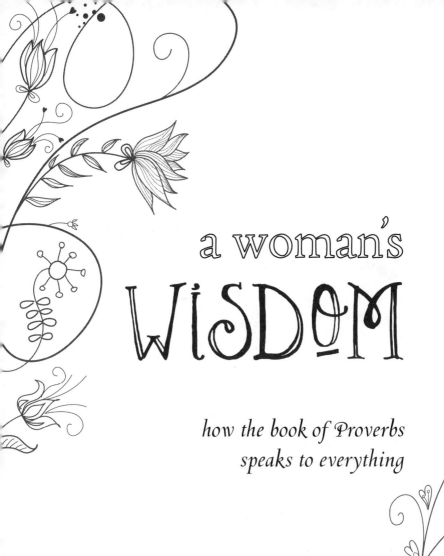

a woman's
WISDOM

how the book of Proverbs
speaks to everything

lydia brownback

:: CROSSWAY

WHEATON, ILLINOIS

A Woman's Wisdom: How the Book of Proverbs Speaks to Everything

Copyright © 2012 Lydia Brownback

Published by Crossway
    1300 Crescent Street
    Wheaton, Illinois 60187

Cover design: Amy Bristow

Cover image(s): Photographer / © Terry Bidgood / Trevillion Images

First printing 2012

Printed in the United States of America

Unless otherwise indicated, Scripture quotations are taken from the ESV® Bible (*The Holy Bible, English Standard Version®*). Copyright © 2001 by Crossway. Used by permission. All rights reserved.

Scripture references marked NKJV are from The New King James Version. Copyright © 1982, Thomas Nelson, Inc. Used by permission.

All emphases in Scripture quotations have been added by the author.

Trade paperback ISBN: 978-1-4335-2827-9

PDF ISBN: 978-1-4335-2828-6

Mobipocket ISBN: 978-1-4335-2829-3

ePub ISBN: 978-1-4335-2830-9

Library of Congress Cataloging-in-Publication Data

Brownback, Lydia, 1963-
   A woman's wisdom : how the book of Proverbs speaks
   to everything / Lydia Brownback.
     p. cm.
   Includes bibliographical references (p. 213) and index.
   ISBN 978-1-4335-2827-9 (tp)
   1. Bible. O.T. Proverbs—Criticism, interpretation, etc.
2. Christian women—Conduct of life. I. Title.
BS1465.53.B76   2012
223'.706—dc23   2011045933

Crossway is a publishing ministry of Good News Publishers.

VP		21	20	19	18	17	16	15	14	13	12
13	12	11	10	9	8	7	6	5	4	3	

With gratitude to God
for
Jamie, Sam, Drew, and Max

May each of you know the blessings of
Wisdom every day of your life.

Blessed is the one who finds wisdom,
and the one who gets understanding,
for the gain from her is better than gain from silver
and her profit better than gold.
She is more precious than jewels,
and nothing you desire can compare with her.

—Proverbs 3:13–15

CONTENTS

PREFACE

What drew you to pick up this book? Most likely, it's that there's something about the idea of wisdom that appeals to you. It just draws your heart.

It is true that there is a certain wisdom that only age can confer, but outside of God and his Word, even that must be suspect. That's because there is no truly reliable wisdom apart from God. To know and trust him *is* wisdom. The way we get this wisdom isn't by living a long time. Nor is it found by trying our best to follow the paths of wisdom that are set before us in the book of Proverbs. Even if we were able to follow those paths, which we are not, we would fail to lay hold of true wisdom. It is found only in Christ,

> for consider your calling . . . not many of you were wise according to worldly standards, not many were powerful, not many were of noble birth. But God chose what is foolish in the world to shame the wise; God chose what is weak in the world to shame the strong; God chose what is low and despised in the world, even things that are not, to bring to nothing things that are, so that no human being might boast in the presence of God. And because of him you are in Christ Jesus, who became to us wisdom from God. (1 Cor. 1:26–30)

preface

Do you know Christ? If you really know him, you belong to him. It couldn't be otherwise. If you get nothing else from reading this book, get this: Christ became for us wisdom from God.

Because the book of Proverbs provides us with a poetic road map of how God has designed the world to work, following its practical day-to-day guidance will surely make your life more pleasant. But disconnected from its divine source, even this will prove hollow in the end. That's what King Solomon, the primary author of Proverbs, found out.

In his better days, King Solomon was indeed the wisest of men. As a young man and newly crowned king, he had prayed for the ability to govern God's people wisely, and God had answered him mightily, so much so that "the whole earth sought the presence of Solomon to hear his wisdom, which God had put into his mind" (1 Kings 10:24). People came from all over the known world to get his advice. Over time, however, Solomon began to give his heart to the worldly rewards of his wisdom rather than to the source of it, and this wisest of all men did some horrendously foolish things. The same thing will happen to us if we try to use Proverbs as a spiritualized means for self-improvement.

Improving our lives is not the objective of Proverbs, even though following its instruction will generally better our lot. The point of the book is to direct us to the Giver of wisdom. Jesus said concerning himself, "The queen of the South will rise up at the judgment with this generation and condemn it, for she came from the ends of the earth to hear the wisdom of Solomon, and behold, something greater than Solomon is here" (Matt. 12:42).

Wisdom is a person, and wise is what we become through our union with him. The outworkings of wisdom—its fruit—discussed in the following chapters are all rooted in this truth. I echo the hopes of the apostle Paul:

That [our] hearts may be encouraged, being knit together in love, to reach all the riches of full assurance of understanding and the knowledge of God's mystery, which is Christ, in whom are hidden all the treasures of wisdom and knowledge. (Col. 2:2–3)

—Lydia Brownback
May 2011

INTRODUCTION

Advice books are no short-lived trend. They continue to top best-seller lists, and new how-to releases get clicked into Amazon shopping carts hundreds of times each day. The popularity of such books isn't likely to wane, even though the "wisdom" of much of what's offered is transient and proves shallow in the long run. How-to books wouldn't be nearly so popular if people would just embrace the wisdom of God's ways, but whenever God's ways—the how-tos of Scripture—are rejected, even shallow alternatives are going to hold appeal.

The problem for so many of us is that we want a formula: three easy steps to the good life. In the midst of meticulously scheduled lives, it is much easier to cruise through the McDonald's drive-thru than to prepare a well-balanced dinner. For the same reason, it is often much easier to digest a quick read on our problem *du jour* than to take time to dig into God's Word. We don't "have time" to get to know him. Maybe tomorrow, we think; today we just want a few pointers on how to minimize stress, balance the budget, and get the kids to behave.

A glance through the book of Proverbs shows us just what we seem to need—short, pithy how-tos in Twitter-like blurbs. However, if we approach Proverbs with a quick-fix mind-set, we are going to miss the overarching point of the book: getting to know and learning to love the Author of wisdom. It is only through knowing and loving God—what Proverbs calls "the fear of the LORD"—that we will understand how to apply its practical how-tos.

We women need practical advice for life, but even more than that, we need hearts set on the One who governs all our practicalities. The book of Proverbs unlocks the key to both. Its wisdom is timeless. Although the book of Proverbs was written to particular people—primarily young men in ancient Israel—its wisdom and the necessity of obtaining it are the same in every age for both men and women. What changes are the circumstances in which to apply it. We may not face the difficulties that ancient women did, but we do face very real challenges:

- practicing biblical womanhood in a world that scorns us for it;
- keeping sexually pure in a sex-saturated society;
- handling our freedom, independence, and material resources wisely;
- maintaining God-glorifying marriages;
- elevating biblical priorities ahead of day-to-day pressures.

Some may be surprised to learn that Proverbs addresses all these things. In fact, there is no area for which we need wisdom that Proverbs doesn't address. That's because all wisdom is summed up this way: "The fear of the LORD is the beginning of wisdom, and the knowledge of the Holy One is insight" (9:10; see also 1:7 NKJV). Once we get this—and embrace it—we will find ourselves equipped to handle the how-tos.

In your hands is a book for women on the wisdom to be gleaned from the book of Proverbs. You will find nine chapters that you can read alone or in a small-group setting with the accompanying study guide at the back of the book. What we will see as we take a close look at Proverbs is that all true wisdom springs from the fear of the Lord.

Part 1, "What Is Wisdom and Why Does It Matter?," is based on chapters 1–3 and 8–9 of Proverbs. Here we will examine why pursuing biblical wisdom, what Proverbs calls "the fear of the LORD," is the primary calling of every Christian woman. Women of wisdom are those who:

- acknowledge God's sovereignty over everything that comes to pass;
- submit to God's ordering of the world;
- cherish Christ above all else;
- trust in the goodness of God's character;
- guard their hearts in biblical truth.

One of the ways that Proverbs shows us the blessings of wisdom is by contrasting wisdom with folly, so we are going to look not only at characteristics of the wise but also at characteristics of fools.

Part 2, "Six Things Wise Women Know," applies biblical wisdom to six aspects of a woman's life: (1) her words; (2) her friendships; (3) her physical appetites; (4) her emotions; (5) her money; and (6) her sexuality.

Part 3, "A Portrait of Wisdom," offers a biblical illustration of all we will study in parts 1 and 2. The focus here is on the woman in Proverbs 31:10–31. Some women are either intimidated by this woman or dismissive of her, but we will see why she isn't at all intimidating. An understanding of how she fits into the overall teaching of Proverbs eliminates any intimidation and can inspire a love of wisdom in specifically feminine ways. May we find ourselves becoming more like her for the good of our families, our churches, and our communities, and for the glory of God.

At the end you'll find a study guide. You can use it on your own as you are reading through the book or for small-group discussion. One of the questions accompanying each chapter is marked with ✭. These questions require more in-depth study and will take a bit longer to complete. If you want more room to interact with the study guide, you can download and print a larger copy for free at crossway.org/awomanswisdom.

> If any of you lacks wisdom, let him ask God, who gives generously to all without reproach, and it will be given him. (James 1:5)

part one

what is wisdom and why does it matter?

CHAPTER 1
what, exactly, is wisdom?

As Christian women living in the twenty-first century, we aren't likely to face many of the tricky difficulties that confronted ancient Israelite women. Just think of Queen Esther, who had to learn how to get along in a harem of women whose only calling was to please the king with their beauty. Even after Esther became queen, the cost of displeasing her king-husband was death. Other Old Testament women dealt with slavery, such as Hagar, and having to share a husband with another woman, such as Rachel and Leah.

Our problems, while less life-threatening for the most part, nevertheless pose tremendous challenges for which we need the same wisdom that ancient women needed. But we want to do more than merely minimize stress and ward off unnecessary difficulties; we also want to please God in every aspect of our lives. This is one way in which biblical wisdom differs radically from worldly wisdom. The world's wisdom centers on how people can please themselves and maximize every pleasure. The wisdom in Proverbs isn't *un*concerned about our enjoying life as a gift from God. That's the beauty of it—as we put into practice the wisdom of Proverbs, we find that

a woman's wisdom

God's ways work at a very practical level; life does tend to run more smoothly. As this happens, God is showcased as the all-wise one, and he is glorified.

That's the wisdom we need. We need it for how to be homemakers in a world that fights us on it. We need it for how to be single when we don't want to be. We need it to live godly lives in a culture of boundless freedoms, independence, and wealth. (Economic hardships in the West do not compare to economic hardships in other parts of the world.) We need the wisdom of Proverbs for how to live biblically when we are immersed in a culture of shallow entertainment options and easy divorce. We need it to make good choices for how to school our kids and for how to navigate our ever-increasing virtual world on the Internet.

We are going to touch on all that, but before we can see how to apply the wisdom of Proverbs to our individual life situations, we need to see exactly what the Bible means by *wisdom*. Where does wisdom come from? Proverbs tells us clearly:

> The fear of the LORD is the beginning of wisdom,
> and the knowledge of the Holy One is insight.
> (Prov. 9:10; see also 1:7)

That, of course, logically leads us to ask, What is the fear of the Lord? Pastors tell us it means "awe," but if that is always what it means, why don't we just use the word *awe*—"awe of the Lord"—instead of the word *fear*? Well, the Hebrew of this word *fear* means both "terror" and "reverence." However, the *terror* part tends to get downplayed because it is hard to reconcile the idea of fear with a loving God. Still, I think we are too quick to discount the terror aspect in "the fear of the LORD." If we look carefully at Scripture, we see that sometimes fear means just that—fear.

Consider the case of the prophet Isaiah, who, after seeing God, said, "Woe is me, for I am undone!" (Isa. 6:5 NKJV). His vision of God" certainly didn't evoke happy feelings.

Then there was Jesus's mother, Mary. When the angel Gabriel came and told her, "Rejoice, highly favored one, the Lord is with you; blessed are you among women," she was troubled at his saying, which led the angel to say to her, "Do not be *afraid*, Mary, for you have found favor with God" (Luke 1:26–30 NKJV).

There is also the example of Moses. When he came upon the burning bush, God called to him from the midst of the bush and said, "Moses, Moses! . . . Take your sandals off your feet, for the place on which you are standing is holy ground." And Moses responded by hiding his face, for "he was *afraid* to look at God" (Ex. 3:4–6). So we see that fear is sometimes awe that is mixed with terror.

What's interesting is that Isaiah, Mary, and Moses all experienced fear as a result of God's drawing near to them. It seems clear that some who have been brought exceptionally near to God have experienced fear in the process. Why is this true, since God is a kind and loving God? Here is why: when sinful people come truly close to God, they see more of who he truly is—holy, as well as loving. In fact, his holiness is part and parcel of his lovingkindness rather than separate from it. The closer we get to God, the more we will see the reality of who he is and who we are in relationship to him. So if you are one of those who has experienced that kind of fear—the terror kind—it should be seen as good news, not bad news, because it is the sort of fear that leads to a true grasp of your need for Christ.

This recognition of our sin before a holy God is what makes us crave a Savior, and when we cast ourselves upon him to fulfill that craving, we will move beyond just merely understanding the doctrines of the Christian faith in our minds to living them from our hearts with deep joy. All this is why the fear of the Lord is the beginning of wisdom. It's because real wisdom is found only in Christ. Wisdom is the realization that he is everything.

After we are driven to Christ through this kind of fear, we can

a woman's wisdom

understand the sort of awe and reverence that pastors use to describe the fear of the Lord. We are able to know God as kind, wise, fatherly, holy, powerful, all-knowing, and compassionate *only in Christ*. It is this view of God that inspires our awe—and our pursuit of wise living or, said another way, holiness. A wise pastor asked us to consider this:

> Is the fear of the Lord a soul-crippling, psyche-damaging conception which our enlightened age has outgrown? The Word of God declares it to be a potent force which purifies and converts the soul from wayward and sinful thoughts and doings (Ps. 19:8, 9). Let us be honest and ask ourselves: How many wicked thoughts and transgressing deeds of ours would have been nipped in the bud had we a right fear of as well as love for our God? A right fear of the Lord is a preventative good. It prevents us from entering into sin, keeps us from nurturing sin, and drives us out of sin when we do fall into it. Positively, the fear of the Lord is the height of wisdom (Ps. 1:7), not a low and damaging superstition.[1]

So, with that in mind, let's look at what it means to live wisely. What is wise living?

To live wisely is to orient everything about ourselves and our lives around God rather than around ourselves. Wise women are God-centered, not self-centered. As we orient ourselves around God, our tastes and interests will change, and we will increasingly love what God loves and hate what he hates:

> The fear of the LORD is hatred of evil. (Prov. 8:13)

To live wisely is also to love righteousness. But do we? If we're honest, we have to admit that, even as Christians, a part of us doesn't hate sin. Why else would we continue to practice it? We hate the horrible effects of the sin we see in our world, in our children, and in our own lives, but we will hate the sin itself only as we grow in the fear of the Lord.

characteristics of wisdom

Now that we have established where real wisdom comes from—the fear of the Lord—we can more fruitfully take a look at some of the particular characteristics of wisdom.

1) Wisdom Is Clear

Wisdom is clear; in other words, it is not hard to find or figure out:

> All the words of my mouth are righteous;
>> there is nothing twisted or crooked in them.
> They are all straight to him who understands,
>> and right to those who find knowledge. (Prov. 8:8–9)

"I've found that to be true for some things," you might be thinking, "but the Bible doesn't provide black-and-white answers for everything. How is wisdom 'straight' when it comes to the gray areas of life?" We are tempted to wonder about that at times, but since it's the Bible that says wisdom's words are all straight, it must be true. The trouble is the way in which we use Scripture to look for wisdom. We want to open our Bibles and find a verse that will correspond directly to our problem and provide a solution. But that's not how we get wisdom. Finding that wisdom is "straight" comes from immersing ourselves in Scripture—all of it, not just a passage here and there—and as we do, it shapes our understanding about all of life. If we make a habit of Scripture immersion, we will find, when confronted with one of life's difficulties, that the wisdom we so desperately need will come to us a lot more easily. Wisdom is indeed clear, but its clarity doesn't come in a three-easy-steps sort of way. The more we soak ourselves in God's Word, the more we will be able to readily lay hold of the wisdom we need for particular circumstances.

Sometimes, despite a thorough soaking in Scripture, much prayer, and the seeking of godly counsel, we still find ourselves perplexed about what to do. But that doesn't mean that biblical wisdom is unclear. It just means that we haven't yet grasped its clarity! At such times, we do well to simply wait for it.

At other times, we ourselves might be blocking our view of the wisdom we need. Once, years ago, Pastor Donald Gray Barnhouse was busily working in his private study when he heard a knock on the door. It was his daughter, and he invited her to enter. She had come to ask his permission to do something that she very much wanted to do. After listening to her, Dr. Barnhouse denied her request and returned his attention to his work. He was startled when he looked up a few minutes later and saw his daughter still standing near his desk. "What are you doing?" he asked.

"I am waiting for you to tell me what to do," she replied.

"Whatever you are doing," he said, "you are not waiting for me to tell you what to do. I have already told you what I want you to do, and you do not like it. What you are really doing is waiting to see if I will change my mind."[2]

Don't we do the same sometimes? At some level, we know what God wants us to do, what the wise course is, but we don't like it, so we default to confusion, claiming that we do not know what to do. If our discovery as to what would please the Lord in a given situation remains elusive, could this be the problem? It's worth investigating. If we find it is so and then repent, we will likely be amazed at how soon we lay hold of the answer we've been after all along.

2) Wisdom Is Near

Not only is wisdom clear, but it is also near. In other words, wisdom is always available:

> Does not wisdom cry out,
>> And understanding lift up her voice?
> She takes her stand on the top of the high hill,
>> Beside the way, where the paths meet.

> She cries out by the gates, at the entry of the city,
>> At the entrance of the doors. (Prov. 8:1–3 NKJV)

God isn't reluctant to give us wisdom. In fact, he delights to make it clear to us:

> Surely I will pour out my spirit on you;
>> I will make my words known to you. (Prov. 1:23 NKJV)

God said through Moses: "This commandment that I command you today is not too hard for you, neither is it far off. It is not in heaven, that you should say, 'Who will ascend to heaven for us and bring it to us, that we may hear it and do it?' Neither is it beyond the sea, that you should say, 'Who will go over the sea for us and bring it to us, that we may hear it and do it?' But the word is very near you. It is in your mouth and in your heart, so that you can do it" (Deut. 30:11–14). We will find it to be "very near" when we do what Moses said just before that: "When you turn to the LORD your God with all your heart and with all your soul . . ." (v. 10). The issue sometimes isn't that we lack wisdom but that we don't really want it.

3) Wisdom Is Pleasant

To say that wisdom is "pleasant" is sort of an understatement. *Pleasant* is a word we associate with life's lesser pleasures, such as a cup of tea on a rainy afternoon—it's nice, but we still wish the sun would come out. Yet the word here in Proverbs isn't meant to convey minimal pleasure. Think of it more in terms of that on-top-of-the-world feeling you get in the middle of one of those rare glitch-free days.

> Her ways are ways of pleasantness,
>> and all her paths are peace. (Prov. 3:17; see also 2:10)

The only way we could ever perceive God's ways to be *un*pleasant is if we are self-centered rather than God-centered, self-seeking rather than Christ-seeking, self-exalting rather than Christ-exalting. It all comes down to whose agenda runs our show.

4) Wisdom Is Primary

Committing ourselves to the pursuit of wisdom is itself a step of wisdom.

> The beginning of wisdom is this: Get wisdom,
> and whatever you get, get insight. (Prov. 4:7)

Wise women are governed by the principles of God's Word, not by their feelings, hormones, or enjoyments. Sounds simple, but it's actually quite difficult, because we tend to collapse the two into one. In other words, we equate wisdom with whatever makes us feel best. We set the compass of our lives toward the happiest-looking circumstances, assuming that doing so is the wisest course. The difficulty is exposed in thinking like this: "It will be better for the kids if we divorce, since we just fight all the time when together." And this: "In order to get emotionally healthy, my counselor says I have to give full vent to my anger." And this: "I've been so depressed lately, so this trip to Belize is a must, even if it makes me late with the mortgage payment." That sort of wisdom does not come from God. It comes from our natural passions. But the more we come to be characterized by the fear of the Lord, the less likely we will be to mistake worldliness for wisdom.

5) Wisdom Is Hospitable

In Proverbs 9 we find an invitation to a dinner party, which Wisdom is hosting. If you're anything like me, this is something you can relate to. Many of us love everything about preparing a special meal for those we love. We take delight in deciding what to serve and how to set the table, and when the day of the party comes, we awaken with anticipation. Before any of this begins, of course, we must issue the invitation. Which special friends will we include? Wisdom's invitation differs from ours in that it goes out to those who aren't yet friends:

> She has slaughtered her beasts; she has mixed her wine;
>   she has also set her table.
> She has sent out her young women to call
>   from the highest places in the town,
> "Whoever is simple, let him turn in here!"
>   To him who lacks sense she says,
> "Come, eat of my bread
>   and drink of the wine I have mixed.
> Leave your simple ways, and live,
>   and walk in the way of insight." (Prov. 9:2–6)

Wisdom invites fools to dinner, and those who RSVP with a *yes* will dine on insight. We find other invitations in Scripture that give us a fuller biblical picture of this invitation in Proverbs. Here is one from the prophet Isaiah: "Come, everyone who thirsts, come to the waters; and he who has no money, come, buy and eat! Come, buy wine and milk without money and without price. Why do you spend your money for that which is not bread, and your labor for that which does not satisfy? Listen diligently to me, and eat what is good, and delight yourselves in rich food" (Isa. 55:1–2). And the fullest picture of all comes from the mouth of Jesus himself: "I am the bread of life; whoever comes to me shall not hunger, and whoever believes in me shall never thirst" (John 6:35).

The full biblical picture reveals that accepting Wisdom's invitation means coming to Christ. The young men who first read the proverbs didn't have the fuller picture that we have, but they understood that following Wisdom leads to life.

how?

As soon as we come to Christ, we're included in the dinner party, and the feasting begins. We have the bread of life. That sounds nice, but what does it mean, exactly, that Jesus is "the bread of life"? We believe it's true, but if we're honest, many of us don't fully understand what it means. Studying Proverbs is a good way to grasp it. The only way to successfully tackle the dos and don'ts of practical wisdom that dominate the book, beginning in the very next chapter (Proverbs 10), is by leaning into and resting all that effort upon Christ, the perfect wise man, who has already "done" wisdom for us.[3] So, as we sit down to partake of Wisdom's feast, we do so leaning on Christ, which is what Jesus meant when he said, "I am the bread of life; whoever comes to me shall not hunger."

Guard Your Heart

The first practical step forward on the path to wisdom involves our hearts:

> Keep your heart with all diligence,
>> for out of it spring the issues of life. (Prov. 4:23 NKJV)

All too often this verse is applied to romantic relationships, which misses the whole point. Certainly it is true that guarding our hearts in a romantic relationship is always wise, but this verse is really about guarding our hearts in the fear of the Lord. If we are going to become increasingly God-centered women, it is essential that we keep a close eye on all that can influence us.

One way to guard our hearts is to be alert to the enticement to sin that comes our way through those who don't fear the Lord:

> Hear, my son, your father's instruction,
>> and forsake not your mother's teaching,
> for they are a graceful garland for your head
>> and pendants for your neck.
> My son, if sinners entice you,
>> do not consent.
> If they say, "Come with us, let us lie in wait for blood;

let us ambush the innocent without reason;
like Sheol let us swallow them alive, and whole,
    like those who go down to the pit;
we shall find all precious goods,
    we shall fill our houses with plunder;
throw in your lot among us;
    we will all have one purse"—
my son, do not walk in the way with them;
    hold back your foot from their paths,
for their feet run to evil,
    and they make haste to shed blood.
For in vain is a net spread in the sight of any bird,
    but these men lie in wait for their own blood;
    they set an ambush for their own lives.
Such are the ways of everyone who is greedy for
        unjust gain;
    it takes away the life of its possessors. (Prov. 1:8–19)

We must be alert to it, but we must also turn away from it. Wise women shun evil counsel; they don't stop to ponder the pros and cons of giving in. That's the mistake Eve made. When the Serpent came to her in the garden of Eden to entice her, she didn't shun his counsel; she lingered and engaged him in conversation about it. And Proverbs 1:8–19 exposes what resides in the hearts of those who follow ungodly paths—greed for the fulfillment of fleshly desires.

Another way we guard our hearts is to be discerning about whose advice we seek and take. This doesn't mean that we shut our ears from ever listening to the advice of an unbeliever. God has equipped all mankind with particular gifts and talents for the good of his creation. If it's medical advice we need, we are wise to seek out the best advice we can get, whether it comes from a believer or an unbeliever. The same is true when it comes to financial advice or guidance concerning real estate or any number of things, so long as the expert has a reputation for integrity. At the same time, expertise aside, wise women will never take any advice that runs counter to biblical principles.

We must be diligent to guard our hearts, because from them "spring the issues of life." The choices we make, for good or ill, are determined by our hearts. Jesus said that "out of the heart come evil thoughts, murder, adultery, sexual immorality, theft, false witness, slander" (Matt. 15:19). It may seem like we are driven to sinful choices through outside influences or adverse circumstances, but it is always and only our hearts that make us sin. As the apostle James wrote, "Each person is tempted when he is lured and enticed by his own desire" (James 1:14).

In light of this, we'd stand no chance were it not for our union with Christ. But in that union, by means of the Holy Spirit who dwells within us, our hearts are progressively transformed, just as Jesus promised: "The water that I will give him will become in him a spring of water welling up to eternal life" (John 4:14). This spring of water wells up and out into godly choices. In order to live wisely, we must choose to do so, and in Christ, we can. Taking the side of folly is therefore unnecessary, and it always results in suffering and regret:

> Because they hated knowledge
> and did not choose the fear of the LORD,
> would have none of my counsel
> and despised all my reproof,
> therefore they shall eat the fruit of their way,
> and have their fill of their own devices. (Prov. 1:29–31)

Cultivate Humility

Another way we grow in wisdom is by cultivating humility. Proverbs 2:6 says that from *God's* mouth, not our mouths, come wisdom and understanding. An attitude of humility recognizes that whatever real wisdom we acquire comes only through our union with Christ. Since Christ is, himself, wisdom from God, how could our wisdom have any other source? When I was twenty years old, I thought I knew everything. When I turned thirty, I realized there were a few things I hadn't quite figured out yet. Not until my forties did I realize that I really know very little. For all of us, it is so often the case that the older we get, the more we realize how little we know, and perhaps this is an indicator that we are finally, by God's grace, beginning to grow in wisdom.

Perhaps you know what I'm talking about from personal experience, or maybe you see it played out in the world around you. Just think about your recent cruises along the highway. Have you noticed that younger folks are inclined to take greater risks while driving? When a car whizzes past us at 85 mph, more often than not the driver, fingers tapping furiously over a handheld miniature keyboard, is under twenty-five years old. Such blatant disregard for driving laws has less to do with a deliberate nose-thumbing at authority than it does with the mistaken belief that nothing will happen to them. But no matter our age, holding to a belief that we're in control of our surroundings or circumstances is the antithesis of humility. Humility looks like this:

> Trust in the LORD with all your heart,
>   and do not lean on your own understanding.
> In all your ways acknowledge him,
>   and he will make straight your paths.
> Be not wise in your own eyes;
>   fear the LORD, and turn away from evil. (Prov. 3:5–7)

Jeremiah was a wise man, but he was also humble, as evidenced from his prayer: "O LORD, I know the way of man is not in himself; it is not in man who walks to direct his own steps" (Jer. 10:23 NKJV). Humility is a prerequisite for wisdom, which is what Jesus was getting at when he said, "Blessed are the poor in spirit, for theirs is the kingdom of heaven" (Matt. 5:3). Trusting in ourselves rather than trusting in the Lord leads inevitably to chaos and confusion, which is why James wrote, "Who is wise and understanding among you? By his good conduct let him show his works in the meekness of wisdom. . . . For where jealousy and selfish ambition exist, there will be disorder and every vile practice" (James 3:13–16). Notice the link James makes between humility (meekness) and godly wisdom. He also makes a link between selfish ambition and worldly wisdom, which leads to demonic chaos. Ongoing disorder in our hearts, minds, and lives may well be a tip-off to an absence of humility.

The psalmist shows us the posture that accompanies all that wise women plan and do: "Behold, as the eyes of servants look to the hand of their master, as the eyes of a maidservant to the hand of her mistress, so our eyes look to the LORD our God" (Ps. 123:2). Proverbs puts it this way:

> My son, do not lose sight of these—
>   keep sound wisdom and discretion,
> and they will be life for your soul
>   and adornment for your neck. (Prov. 3:21–22)

As disciples of Christ, we are servants of God, and as servants, we keep our eyes on him and receive our instructions through his Word. Recognizing our servant status is the essence of wisdom.

Acknowledge God's Sovereignty

Acknowledging God's sovereignty over everything goes hand-in-hand with humility, because only when both are present in our hearts will we depend on God. Practicing the fear of the Lord—living in wisdom—recognizes that God is in control of everything, from the election of presidents to the affairs of our personal lives. When we are young, still living at home with our parents, we begin to dream about how we want our lives to go, and we start to plan how to make those dreams come true. Additionally, we are encouraged from an early age to set goals, so we do. And since we live in a culture where achieving personal goals has been comparatively easy, we are prone to disappointment when our plans don't work out. Inevitably, one or more of our goals is going to get derailed. A young woman goes off to college fully expecting that she will be engaged by graduation, or accepted into a good program for a post-graduate degree, or wind up with the job of her dreams. When some—or all, as the case may be—of those plans fail to materialize, the college graduate feels bewildered and wonders where things went wrong.

Many of us have lived long enough to know that goals are better termed *hopes*, since we have seen many of our best-laid plans go astray. Over time we might come to think of what we wind up doing as a sort of Plan B. But the truth is that there is no Plan B. There is only Plan A. That's because

> The plans of the heart belong to man,
>> but the answer of the tongue is from the LORD.
>> (Prov. 16:1)

If we think we are stuck in Plan B, it's because our idea of Plan A was just that—our own idea, not God's. God has good purposes for us, whether he accomplishes them through the goals we set or through thwarting those goals and leading us along paths we hadn't planned on. We may not be able to discern his purposes, but Proverbs teaches us that we can rest assured that he has them and that he is overseeing the fulfillment of them:

> The heart of man plans his way,
>> but the LORD establishes his steps. (Prov. 16:9)

And

> The king's heart is in the hand of the LORD,
>> Like the rivers of water;
>> He turns it wherever He wishes. (Prov. 21:1 NKJV)

What happened to the prophet Jonah is a good illustration of how God works sovereignly in the lives of his people. God instructed

Jonah to go to Nineveh with a message of coming judgment, but Jonah didn't like God's plan, so he embarked on a plan of his own design by boarding a ship for Tarshish. Many of us know what happened: a big storm arose, and eventually Jonah was tossed overboard and swallowed by a large fish. There, in the belly of the fish, Jonah repented of his willfulness. Afterward the fish vomited him onto dry land, and from there Jonah proceeded to Nineveh.

Jonah's missionary work in Nineveh might have been Plan B so far as Jonah was concerned, but because it was God's plan, it had always been Plan A. God got Jonah where he wanted him, despite Jonah's attempts to run away, and God does the same thing with us. Our response doesn't change the outcome, any more than it did with Jonah; it merely determines whether the way there will be easy or hard.

Wisdom helps us to shape our plans in keeping with God's ways, which in turn keeps us from vainly spinning our wheels; and it spares us and others the frustration that inevitably results when plans are made and pursued with little or no knowledge of God. Then, if things don't go as we had hoped, wisdom enables us to live contentedly in his sovereign ordering of the details of our lives.

Actively Pursue It

Although wisdom is near to us and not too hard to understand, we must actively pursue it. Just consider the active verbs in this passage:

> My son, if you *receive* my words
>   and *treasure up* my commandments with you,
> *making* your ear attentive to wisdom
>   and *inclining* your heart to understanding;
> yes, if you *call out* for insight
>   and *raise your voice* for understanding,
> if you *seek it* like silver
>   and *search for it* as for hidden treasures,

then you will understand the fear of the LORD
and find the knowledge of God. (Prov. 2:1–5)

We may think that receiving God's words is a passive action, something we sit back to read and absorb while sipping a mug of coffee, but
if you look at how the passage is structured, you will see that making
our ears attentive, inclining our hearts, calling out, raising our voices,
seeking, and searching are all part of how we grow in wisdom.

Obey

We also grow wise by obedience. In fact, seeking to live in obedience to God's Word is a necessary heart attitude for all who wish to
be wise:

My son, keep my words
and treasure up my commandments with you;
keep my commandments and live;
keep my teaching as the apple of your eye. (Prov. 7:1–2)

Obedience and wisdom go hand in hand because obeying God is
always wise. As we pursue a lifestyle of obedience, it will lead us to a
deeper understanding of why obeying all God's ways is the best path.
It will also lead to a greater depth of obedience, which will enrich
both our walk with the Lord and our enjoyment of day-to-day life.

Accept God's Discipline

Growing in wisdom also entails recognizing and accepting God's
discipline:

Do not despise the LORD's discipline,
or be weary of his reproof. (Prov. 3:11)

Job, at the beginning of his hard time, shows us how to live out
Proverbs 3:11. After Job lost his livelihood and his children and

was struck with painful boils all over his body, his wife said to him, "Do you still hold to your integrity? Curse God and die!" (Job 2:9 NKJV). But Job rebuked her for her lack of wisdom, saying, "You speak as one of the foolish women speaks. Shall we indeed accept good from God, and shall we not accept adversity?" (v. 10 NKJV). Job's submission to God's work in his life is a hallmark of wisdom.

We tend to think of God's discipline as being the same as how we discipline our kids: they misbehave, and we punish them to teach them that a particular misbehavior is destructive. God's discipline of us, however, is often not linked to some specific wrongdoing on our part. When things go wrong in our lives, we are tempted to try to hunt up what we might have done to cause the difficulty. It is true that sometimes a particular trouble is God's way of pointing out a particular sin we have been ignoring or refusing to repent of, but if no connection is made evident, we don't have to wrack our brains to dig up something. If there's a connection, God is able to make it clear. If no connection is evident, we can simply trust God in the midst of our difficulty and focus on this truth:

> It is for discipline that you have to endure. God is treating you as sons. For what son is there whom his father does not discpline? If you are left without discpline, in which all have participated, then you are illegitimate children and not sons. Besides this, we have had earthly fathers who discplined us and we respected them. Shall we not much more be subect to the Father of spirits and live? For they disciplined us for a short time as it seemed best to them, but he disciplines us for our good, that we may share his holiness. (Heb. 12:7–10)

Rest in Christ

Cultivating such wisdom would be an impossible task were it not for the primary means through which it comes—abiding in Christ. The wisest women are those who have discovered that wisdom and its fruits come most fully to those who seek them not in themselves but in another. Jesus said, "Come to me, all who labor and are heavy laden, and I will give you rest. Take my yoke upon you, and learn from me, for I am gentle and lowly in heart, and you will find rest for your souls" (Matt. 11:28–29). The yoke Jesus had in mind was a plowing device. Once placed around the neck of an animal and hitched to the plow, the animal could move only where the cart driver directed. But, unlike the farmer with his oxen, Jesus doesn't force us to wear his yoke; he invites us. If we accept his invitation, we are going to learn his ways as he steers us along paths of his choosing, and as we do, we are promised to find rest.

benefits of wise living

The benefits of wise living are too numerous to include in a single book, but let's look at a few of them. Women who live wisely will experience, first, *security*. Wise women are confident that they rest on safe ground:

> You will walk on your way securely,
> and your foot will not stumble.
> If you lie down, you will not be afraid;
> when you lie down, your sleep will be sweet.
> (Prov. 3:23–24)

Wise women have no fear. Because they trust God, they have no need for anxiety. They are confident that a kind, wise God is in control of everything. As wisdom increases, anxiety decreases. What makes you worry? Is it finances, your kids, your spouse—or the lack of one? Wise women know that God is trustworthy and that he can and will handle all these matters for our good and his glory.

Another result of wise living is *guidance*. Some time ago I heard someone say that wisdom isn't so much something that God

a woman's wisdom

gives to us as something he *does* for us, a truth reinforced by this passage:

> For the LORD gives wisdom;
>   from his mouth come knowledge and understanding;
> he stores up sound wisdom for the upright;
>   he is a shield to those who walk in integrity,
> guarding the paths of justice
>   and watching over the way of his saints. (Prov. 2:6–8)

The link between wisdom and guidance is also made crystal clear in this proverb:

> Trust in the LORD with all your heart,
>   and do not lean on your own understanding.
> In all your ways acknowledge him,
>   and he will make straight your paths. (Prov. 3:5–6).

This does not mean that God's guidance is conditional upon our trusting; he is always actively directing the lives of human beings. Yet it is only as we actively trust God and submit to his ways that we experience his guidance as a straight path, one not filled with frustrating self-made detours, as we saw with Jonah.

Another benefit of wisdom is the calm enjoyment of *sanctified common sense*. There is no issue in life that Scripture doesn't somehow address. Situations arise in all of our lives that Scripture doesn't directly speak to—those gray areas. But the Bible does address them somehow, even if indirectly, and wisdom is what enables us to use the Word to make black-and-white application into the gray places of our lives. Wisdom enables us to better discern not only what God's Word says explicitly but also what the Word says implicitly, and we are increasingly equipped to apply its truths to all areas of life. Sanctified common sense is the result of wisdom.

Still another result of wise living is *generally good living*:

My son, do not forget my teaching,
　　but let your heart keep my commandments,
for length of days and years of life
　　and peace they will add to you. (Prov. 3:1–2)

The book of Proverbs reveals to us how God has designed the world to work; so, in general, those who live according to God's design prosper because of it. That being said, the proverbs aren't a guarantee for the good life. We all experience times when things don't go well, despite our efforts to follow God's ways, and that's because God has as much to teach us through suffering as he does through blessing us with the practical benefits of wisdom. That's why it is best to view the proverbs as observations or principles rather than as promises. We must keep both things—the practical benefits of wise living and the spiritual benefits of suffering—in tension, and trust that God knows what he is doing in each case.

That being said, we tend to be suspect of this whole idea of delighting in prosperous living. It just seems so, well, worldly. But God delights to bless his children, as any good father does. When God blesses us with a season of prosperity, we can grieve God's father heart if we bar ourselves from rejoicing in it. After years of saving money for a house, a friend of mine was blessed to be able to purchase a lovely home. But she couldn't fully enjoy it because, she said, "I keep waiting for the ax to drop. If God has given me this, what is he preparing to take away?" Such thinking robs both God and us of taking pleasure in his gifts. If he blesses us in some material way, we are free to enjoy it. As Solomon wrote, "There is nothing better for a person than that he should eat and drink and find enjoyment in his toil. This also, I saw, is from the hand of God" (Eccles. 2:24).

Another benefit of acquiring wisdom is *happiness*:

Blessed is the one who finds wisdom,
　　and the one who gets understanding,
for the gain from her is better than gain from silver

> and her profit better than gold.
> She is more precious than jewels,
> and nothing you desire can compare with her.
> (Prov. 3:13–15)

Can you think of a better definition for *happiness*? If we are unhappy Christians, the problem isn't our circumstances; it's our interpretation of our circumstances, an interpretation that's lacking in wisdom. Even unhappy occasions can be experienced with joy and peace when we remember who has ordained them and that he has done so for good reason. Wise women know that lasting and deep happiness will never be found in circumstances but only in Wisdom, which is Christ.

One more fruit of wisdom is *self-knowledge*. John Calvin said that before we can know ourselves, we must first know God. Only God really knows and understands our hearts, of course, but the better we know God, the better we will know ourselves. Self-knowledge, part and parcel of which is awareness of our personal weaknesses, is vital when it comes to resisting temptations, since temptations appeal to us in areas where we tend to be weak. Women who know God are better able to recognize where they are prone to sin and are therefore better equipped to deal with it intelligently. Knowing ourselves is a benefit of wisdom.

> In vain is a net spread
> in the sight of any bird. (Prov. 1:17)

our wisdom

All of this leaves us with a problem: we can't do it! Who among us could ever hope to achieve wisdom such as we see in Proverbs? Wisdom is indeed impossible for us, even though, after glimpsing the benefits of it, we want to become wise women. What are we to do? The realization of our impossible dilemma brings Paul's words to life: "God chose what is low and despised in the world, even things that are not, to bring to nothing things that are, so that no human being might boast in the presence of God. And because of him you are in Christ Jesus, who became to us wisdom from God" (1 Cor. 1:28–30). Christ is our wisdom, in both its characteristics and benefits. We have no wisdom of our own, but if we are in him, we have his wisdom, which means we can grow it to fullness. In Christ "are hidden all the treasures of wisdom and knowledge" (Col. 2:3). If we are in Christ, those treasures are ours too.

CHAPTER 2
why folly is really bad

A young couple walks hand in hand into the jewelry store. The girl's face is aglow with happiness. The young man looks happy too, but he also gives off a bit of nervous anxiety. His girl has just said yes to his marriage proposal, and they have come in to buy an engagement ring. The jeweler, who has seen dozens of couples walk through his doors, knows from first glance why they have come. As he greets the couple, he unlocks the glass case inside of which are nestled rows of diamond rings—oval, emerald, marquis, and princess—and whisks onto the counter a black velvet display square. He knows that the sparkle of the rings shows most brightly against the contrasting dark background of the velvet.

The book of Proverbs does something similar. Its authors knew that wisdom is seen in the light of full splendor when displayed against the darkness of folly. A foolish woman is the opposite of a wise woman. A foolish woman is not necessarily one lacking intellectual capabilities; in fact, from an intellectual standpoint, she might be one of the brightest women around. So what makes her foolish?

> The heart of him who has understanding seeks knowledge,
> but the mouths of fools feed on folly. (Prov. 15:14)

Unlike a wise woman, a foolish one does not fear the Lord. She doesn't submit to God but seeks to live unencumbered by any rule or authority that thwarts her desires. She feeds on arrogance rather than on humility, as we will see here in this quick overview, and later throughout the book.

traits of a foolish woman

The dark threads of folly are woven throughout the thirty-one chapters of Proverbs, and, as we will note, these dark threads can entangle us spiritually, emotionally, physically, and materially.

She Is Easily Enticed by the World

Proverbs shows us that a foolish woman is one easily enticed by the world. We see her in the woman who buys into the lie that looking young and beautiful is the path to fulfillment. Anyone who believes that has been ensnared by folly. Such a woman devotes the best of her resources—time and money—to her appearance. Her belief in the sparkling but false promises of physical beauty will prevent her from enjoying the freedom of aging gracefully.

> In everything the prudent acts with knowledge,
> but a fool flaunts his folly. (Prov. 13:16).

A woman easily enticed by the world is also materialistic and ambitious for worldly success. She is intrigued by worldly philosophies and allows them to shape her understanding about everything. For such a woman, self-esteem and self-worth can seem to her more valuable than following Christ in a lifestyle of self-denial.

She Trusts in Riches

A foolish woman believes the lie that material blessings can be gained apart from God.

> Whoever trusts in his riches will fall,
> > but the righteous will flourish like a green leaf.
> > (Prov. 11:28)

Such a woman disregards the warning of Proverbs 1:

> If sinners entice you,
> > do not consent.
> If they say, . . .
> "we shall find all precious goods,
> > we shall fill our houses with plunder;
> throw in your lot among us;
> > we will all have one purse"—
> my son, do not walk in the way with them;
> > hold back your foot from their paths. (Prov. 1:10–15)

Temptation to acquire more and more rarely comes at us in such an obvious way. More often, it lurks in the shadows and twists last night's dinner with a friend into a legitimate business expense or convinces us that it's not wrong to rack up credit card debt for a new sofa.

She Is Proud and Hates Knowledge

A foolish woman hates knowledge. She is one who shuns, ignores, disdains, scorns, or rationalizes away biblical wisdom and counsel. She lives by the dictates of her emotions, and she insists on fulfilling her personal desires and believes that her way of thinking is always the right way. To such a woman Proverbs asks:

> How long, O simple ones, will you love being simple?
> How long will scoffers delight in their scoffing
> > and fools hate knowledge? (Prov. 1:22)

a woman's wisdom

The foolish woman is proud, and she is a scoffer. Proverbs indicates that *scoffing* is a refusal to embrace God's ways—hanging onto that one secret sin, that one relationship, that one bad habit, that one questionable indulgence.

Despite the warnings God sends through his Word and his people, scoffers never really get what they seek, and wisdom will laugh in their face:

> Because you have ignored all my counsel
>> and would have none of my reproof,
> I also will laugh at your calamity;
>> I will mock when terror strikes you. (Prov. 1:25–26)

Put more simply, a scoffer, someone characterized and dominated by pride, will inevitably taste great regret. We may not be full-blown scoffers, but we all, without exception, are tainted by the folly of pride. Whenever we blame God for something, we can be sure we are proud. Whenever we think we don't have a problem with pride, we have a problem with pride. Any time the knowledge of God and his ways is scorned, pride lies at the root of it.

She Is Complacent

A foolish woman is complacent, which, in this context, means she is contented with a mediocre Christian life. She fails to grasp the truth that there is no middle road, no fence-sitting, when it comes to discipleship; we are at all times either going forward or going backward. That's why living in limbo is really only an illusion.

Certainly there are times, such as when we are faced with a difficult decision or a perplexing problem, when sitting still for a season is more constructive than throwing all our energies at a quick solution. That sort of limbo is wise because it gives us time to seek God's leading from Scripture and to get advice from others. The limbo of complacency, on the other hand, isn't characterized by seeking. Instead, it is characterized by a desire to do nothing more than escape an uncomfortable situation or avoid making a decision. The limbo of complacency is comfortable at first, and often it feels like the safest place to be. There seem to be no risks, whereas to enter wholeheartedly into one particular course or another just feels too scary; after all, we have no guarantee of how things will turn out. But avoidance is actually unsafe. Proverbs is very clear on the danger of complacency:

> The simple are killed by their turning away,
>   and the complacency of fools destroys them. (Prov. 1:32)

She Is Lazy

A foolish woman is also lazy. Proverbs advises us to think about how ants live:

> Go to the ant, O sluggard;
>   consider her ways, and be wise.
>
> Without having any chief,
>   officer, or ruler,
> she prepares her bread in summer
>   and gathers her food in harvest. (Prov. 6:6–8)

As we look at these ants, we recognize the wisdom of working hard at our particular callings, whether that be homemaking, full-time ministry, or a career. But the principle of industriousness applies equally to spiritual matters and to every other area of our lives. Proverbs sounds a cry to exercise ourselves toward wisdom and good judgment in all our ways and relationships. A lazy woman has no zeal, and her folly is revealed in her refusal to fight against indwelling sin and to live for the glory of God. Underlying much of her struggle with laziness is often a refusal to give up personal comforts.

She Is Sinfully Independent

A foolish woman is sinfully independent. In other words, she seeks autonomy from God and others. To her Proverbs says:

> Whoever isolates himself seeks his own desire;
>   he breaks out against all sound judgment. (Prov. 18:1)

Foolish independence disregards advice. When we dig in our heels against biblically sound advice, it is typically because we are concerned only with what we want and with our own perceptions. I have witnessed this very scenario with Abby. For months Abby's friends have expressed concern about her romance with Pete. Over time, the relationship has pulled Abby away from her pursuit of spiritual things, and the light has gone out of her eyes. Pete doesn't treat her with gentle care or respect. Abby's friends have seen all this and have voiced their concerns to Abby, but in response she either changes the subject or tells them everything is fine. Deep down she knows they are right, but Abby has been ensnared by folly. If she persists, her heart will grow hard, and she is likely to waste weeks, months, or years in a destructive romantic relationship simply because the immediate, usually short-lived, pain of a breakup is too difficult to contemplate.

how to recognize a fool

As we consider how Proverbs defines foolish character, we might already have in mind a friend who could well benefit from some serious time in this portion of Scripture. Very likely, there are several friends or acquaintances we have mentally pegged. If we want to be wise, however, we won't devote ourselves to pegging others as fools. We will look instead at ourselves. We cannot know the hearts of others, and we are utterly dependent on God to discern correctly anything about ourselves. Jesus's conversation with the disciples at the Last Supper makes that clear. Jesus said, "'Truly, I say to you, one of you will betray me, one who is eating with me.' They began to be sorrowful and to say to him one after another, 'Is it I?'" (Mark 14:18–19). It's interesting that not one of them asked, "Is it Judas?"[1]

Nevertheless, in dependence on the Holy Spirit and God's Word, moving away from folly and toward wisdom begins with self-examination. Are we foolish women or wise? Let's examine ourselves in light of this list in Proverbs of things God hates:

> There are six things that the LORD hates,
>   seven that are an abomination to him:
> haughty eyes, a lying tongue,
>   and hands that shed innocent blood,
> a heart that devises wicked plans,
>   feet that make haste to run to evil,
> a false witness who breathes out lies,
>   and one who sows discord among brothers.
>   (Prov. 6:16–19)

We may think we aren't fools until we realize that haughty eyes are walking into someone's home and taking pleasure because we have better taste in décor or because our outfit is more appropriate for the occasion. We may think we don't shed innocent blood until we remember Jesus's words that anger is murder. We may think we don't stir up trouble unless we realize that we do so by participating in gossip. Each one of us is, in some way, a foolish woman.

Proverbs doesn't sugarcoat the outcome of folly. The end of a fool is terrible indeed, and recognizing that we are numbered among fools can be quite discouraging. As we noted earlier, foolish women will hear wisdom laughing (Prov. 1:26). Perhaps you have heard that laugh. It is echoed in the why-oh-whys and the if-onlys:

"If only I hadn't done that!"

"Why did I go there!"

"If only I hadn't eaten that!"

"Why did I listen to him!"

"If only I hadn't bought that!"

Fools, according to Proverbs,

> shall eat the fruit of their way,
> and have their fill of their own desires. (Prov. 1:31)

Christ our wisdom

So where does that leave us? Wisdom cries aloud for our attention, but so does folly, and because we are inherently sinful, folly doesn't have to shout as loudly. What are we to do? Again, the remedy is found not so much in exercising ourselves in wise principles but primarily in resting in the source of wisdom: "Christ the power of God and the wisdom of God" (1 Cor. 1:24). Christ is the foolish woman's remedy. That is how we are meant to apply this proverb:

> Leave your simple ways, and live,
> and walk in the way of insight. (Prov. 9:6)

It bears repeating that overcoming folly and growing in wisdom simply aren't about culling advice from the book of Proverbs, as if it were the biblical version of *How to Win Friends and Influence People*. Apart from Christ, the earthly blessings that flow from right living are merely a shadow of the real thing. From the Bible's viewpoint, wise living and its fruit are impossible apart from Christ because the fear of the Lord—Proverbs' definition of wisdom—is known only to those who are in Christ. If we eat of this bread and drink of the living water he offers, we will know increasingly the wisdom that banishes the folly that clings to us today.

part two
six things wise women know

the world . . .

Lying is very stressful. It actually can make you feel really worthless—a crutch you get in the habit of using when you really don't need one. But because lies beget other lies, you start to think that who you really are does need all that cover-up, so you end up with very little faith in yourself. We need to get you out of this rut. There's a golden rule that you need to embrace if you want to stop lying: There is nothing and no one that is better than you.

—*Seventeen* magazine

the word . . .

Lying lips are an abomination to the LORD,
but those who act faithfully are his delight.

—Proverbs 12:22

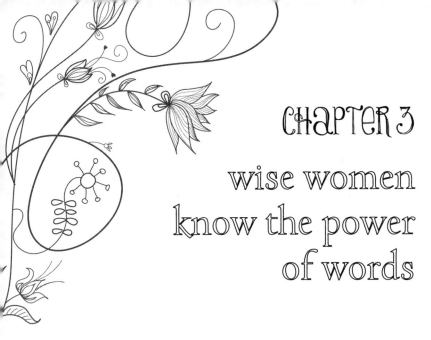

CHAPTER 3

wise women know the power of words

Our words carry tremendous power, and perhaps that is why Proverbs contains so many sayings about how we use our tongues.

> Death and life are in the power of the tongue,
> and those who love it will eat its fruits. (Prov. 18:21)

And

> A fool's mouth is his ruin,
> and his lips are a snare to his soul. (Prov. 18:7)

We find the same perspective in the New Testament. The apostle James wrote, "The tongue is a fire, a world of unrighteousness. The tongue is set among our members, staining the whole body, setting on fire the entire course of life, and set on fire by hell. For every kind of beast and bird, of reptile and sea creature, can be tamed and has been tamed by mankind, but no human being can tame the tongue. It is a restless evil, full of deadly poison. With it we bless our Lord and Father, and with it we curse people who are made in the likeness of

God" (James 3:6–9). So it is clear that we can greatly affect our well-being and that of others by what we do with our tongues.

That being said, the power of our words springs not from our actual tongue but from the heart that controls it. Jesus made clear that our words are a reflection of our hearts, which is why they will be judged so strictly: "The good person out of his good treasure brings forth good, and the evil person out of his evil treasure brings forth evil. I tell you, on the day of judgment people will give account for every careless word they speak, for by your words you will be justified, and by your words you will be condemned" (Matt. 12:35–37).

helping words

As we've seen, the proverbs were originally recorded to instruct young men in God's ways, but the truths we find in them aren't just applicable to young men. They are fitting for everyone—male or female, young or old—because they are God's truths. There is, however, a distinction in how to apply them.

God designed women to complement men. That's not *compliment* with an *i* but *complement* with an *e*. That one letter makes all the difference. To complement means to fill up, complete, or make perfect. That's what God had in mind when he said, "It is not good that the man should be alone; I will make him a helper fit for him" (Gen. 2:18). Actually, it's a two-way street; men and women were designed to complement each other. Men and women have been hardwired with distinctive gender traits that, when working together, serve the human race and display the glory of God.

The word *helper* gets a bad rap. In the marriage context it can conjure up a mental picture of a worn-out wife trudging through the housework and seeking to help her man accomplish his personal goals while he has a stimulating day at the office. But that is not what God had in mind. A wife's calling is to help her husband accomplish *God's* goals. The two working together, each with particular strengths, grow and build up God's family and spread God's name throughout the world.

There is actually a lot of power in being a helper, because one of the primary ways we exercise it is by influence, and we influence by means of our words. All that to say, one of the primary ways we fulfill our role as helper is through our tongues. A godly helper uses her words to build up, to encourage, and to disseminate God's Word.

A woman who used her tongue for the good of others was Esther. In fact, she risked her life in doing so after her relative Mordecai said, "Do not think in your heart that you will escape in the king's palace any more than all the other Jews. For if you remain completely silent at this time, relief and deliverance will arise for the Jews from another place, but you and your father's house will perish. Yet who knows whether you have come to the kingdom for such a time as this?" (Est. 4:13–14 NKJV). The Jews of her day were up against a secretive deadly plot, but because Esther employed her tongue with great wisdom, the Jews were saved.

We can, however, corrupt the call to help, to influence for good, by our words. Consider Delilah in Judges 16. Delilah was a Philistine woman who was employed by her countrymen to trick the Israelite judge Samson. From what we are given to see of Samson in the Bible, it is apparent that he was susceptible to worldly women like Delilah. She put to use all of her feminine wiles—including her speech—to convince Samson to reveal the secret of his great strength so that the Philistines might come in and overpower him. On three separate occasions Delilah said, "Please tell me where your great strength lies, and how you might be bound, that one could subdue you" (v. 6). Because Samson was infatuated with this woman, he believed she was merely playing some sort of lovers' game, and he teased her with wrong answers time and again. Finally, though, when Delilah's manipulative words failed to charm the secret from Samson, she nagged the truth from him, harassing him verbally until he gave in from sheer frustration.

Delilah epitomizes how a woman can misuse her tongue to destroy. God hasn't given us the gift of speech to gratify our selfish desires. It is meant for building up, encouraging, and setting forth wisdom. When a woman uses her tongue to influence for good, God is glorified and the people in her life are blessed. Will we use our words to manipulate for selfish gain? Or will we use them for the good of others? We will face this choice every day in every conversation we have.

words of folly

If we isolate all the proverbs that have to do with our words, we find that certain speech sins are addressed repeatedly, so of these we should take careful note.

Lies

From Proverbs we learn a lot about the characteristics of a liar and the consequences of lying. One thing we learn is that lying is futile because it is always caught and punished:

> A false witness will not go unpunished,
>> and he who breathes out lies will not escape. (Prov. 19:5)

Sometimes we lie because we feel cornered; it's almost a knee-jerk response to avoid shame or embarrassment. Other times our lies might be more deliberate. Either way, Proverbs indicates that liars will be held accountable for their words.

We also discover that there is a link between hatred and lying:

> The one who conceals hatred has lying lips,
>> and whoever utters slander is a fool. (Prov. 10:18)

> A lying tongue hates its victims,
>> and a flattering mouth works ruin. (Prov. 26:28)

wise women know the power of words

As we can see, hatred and lying go together. Lying expresses contempt for the one being lied to. It is a move away from relationship. Recall a time when someone lied to you, and think about why it hurt when you found out. Chances are it wasn't just whatever the liar had tried to cover up but also the fact that the liar created a barrier in your relationship. The act of lying is a maneuvering tactic for creating relational distance, whether or not the liar is conscious of doing so.

Another thing we learn from Proverbs about lying is how much God hates it:

> There are six things that the LORD hates,
>   seven that are an abomination to him:
> haughty eyes, a lying tongue,
>   and hands that shed innocent blood. (Prov. 6:16–17)

> Lying lips are an abomination to the LORD,
>   but those who act faithfully are his delight.
>   (Prov. 12:22; 6:17)

Abomination is a pretty strong word. In Scripture it is attached to behaviors for which God has a particular disgust and loathing. For that reason, wise women also hate lying:

> The righteous hates falsehood,
>   but the wicked brings shame and disgrace. (Prov. 13:5)

To hate something is to reject it, to utterly repudiate it, and to cringe when it confronts us. Wise women take honest speech seriously and do not consider half-truths, white lies, or anger-generated vows as legitimate exceptions. If we catch ourselves telling a lie, we stop and tell the truth. Those who are careful to speak only truth are trusted and their words are weighty, whereas those who are careless with the truth aren't taken seriously.

Ellie learned this firsthand with her daughter Kate, who had been pushing the boundaries of her curfew for several weeks. Ellie warned Kate that if she broke curfew again, she would be grounded. It did happen again, that very week, but Ellie didn't follow through with the punishment. As a result, Kate has lost respect for her mother and gives even less weight to Ellie's rules.

If we want to be taken seriously, and if we really want to love those around us, we won't be careless with the truth. When a friend asks if we think she needs to lose weight, we will tell her the truth rather than just what will make her feel good at the moment. If a coworker tells us she is planning to use a sick day for fun at the beach, we don't back up her dishonesty with our own untruth and say, "Hey, that's okay. You need a break." Being scrupulous with the truth can be hard sometimes, but the payoff is worth it.

What about things like Santa Claus and keeping surprise parties a secret? It is possible to participate in the delights of such occasions without lying. I think, for example, of the husband of a friend of mine who recently threw his wife a surprise birthday party. He worked behind the scenes to gather her friends for the occasion and managed to keep the party planning so completely off her radar that he never once felt cornered into having to lie.

When it comes to Christmas, some Christian parents include Santa in their family tradition and others do not. Among those who do, I've known many who incorporate Santa without actually leading their children to believe that the gifts under the tree were left there by a jolly old man who came down the chimney. However Santa is handled in your home, it provides an opportunity to teach children about wise words as they are exposed to those whose Christmas tradition differs from theirs.

Surprise parties, Santa Claus, and sensitivity to others' feelings are just some of the areas in which bringing joy to another without compromising truth can take some creativity, but since God is the originator of joy and truth, he will surely help us to convey both in these situations, if we ask him to.

Wise women take to heart all Proverbs has to say about the inevitable destruction of lying, the reality of which is played out before us all the time. The demise of the political career of John Edwards is a recent illustration. When the media exposed his extramarital affair with a staffer, he initially denied the reports, but as evidence of his infidelity grew, he had no choice but to admit the truth that he not only had been unfaithful to his wife but also had fathered a child through the affair. His lies harmed numerous people—dedicated political supporters, both his illegitimate child and legitimate children, and his wife, who had been diagnosed with cancer at the time of the scandal. His wife, Elizabeth, stuck by her husband until the depth of his attempted cover-up became known. Elizabeth Edwards died some time ago, and although John was in the family home at the time of her death, the media reported that she had cut John from her estate just days before. Those he harmed will be scarred certainly, but in time it is to be hoped that what he did and tried to cover up won't prove detrimental to their lives. Not so with John himself. In the eyes of the public, at least, he will be remembered not as a great politician but as a liar.

False Witness

Another speech folly found in Proverbs is false witness, of which lying is a subset.

> A faithful witness does not lie,
> > but a false witness breathes out lies. (Prov. 14:5)

We also find it in the ninth commandment: "You shall not bear false witness against your neighbor" (Ex. 20:16). When we encounter this commandment, a courtroom scene pops into our minds. We picture a court officer placing a Bible before a witness and asking, "Do you swear to tell the truth, the whole truth, and nothing but the truth—so help you God?" But not bearing false witness includes more than being truthful in court. What exactly is false witness? The term is broader than simple lying, as the Westminster Larger Catechism points out:

> The duties required in the ninth commandment are, the preserving and promoting of truth between man and man, and the good name of our neighbor, as well as our own; appearing and standing for the truth; and from the heart, sincerely, freely, clearly, and fully, speaking the truth, and only the truth, in matters of judgment and justice, and in all things whatsoever; a charitable esteem of our neighbors; loving, desiring, and rejoicing in their good name; sorrowing for, and covering of their infirmities; freely acknowledging of their gifts and graces, defending their innocency; a ready receiving of a good report, and unwillingness to admit of an evil report, concerning them; discouraging talebearers, flatterers, and slanderers; love and care of our own good name, and defending it when need requireth; keeping of lawful promises; studying and practicing of whatsoever things are true, honest, lovely, and of good report.[1]

It seems, then, that we break the ninth commandment every time we sin with our tongue! Any speech sin breaks the ninth commandment.

The Westminster Catechism points out something interesting: we can bear false witness against ourselves. We do this whenever we put ourselves down. "I'm such an idiot!" we say, when the good china platter slips from our grasp and smashes on the floor. We also bear false witness against ourselves when we focus perpetually on our weaknesses rather than view ourselves through the lens of God's Word. We need a healthy self-image, the world says, but this is only possible if it is shaped by God's Word. A healthy self-image is found in reflecting God's image. The world tells us to glory in our particular strengths, in what makes us measure up to or surpass the accomplishments of others. The Bible, on the other hand, tells us to rejoice that we have been made in the image of our Creator. A truly healthy self-image can be glimpsed in the words of the psalmist: "You formed my inward parts; you knitted me together in my mother's womb. I praise you, for I am fearfully and wonderfully made. Wonderful are your works; my soul knows it very well" (Ps. 139:13–14).

Concerning our neighbor, bearing false witness can be as much about what we don't say as it is about what we do say. We bear false witness whenever we refuse to stand up and defend someone who is being gossiped about in our presence (more on this below). We can also bear false witness against our neighbor in our hearts when we presume to pass judgment on her intentions or motives.

> A man who bears false witness against his neighbor
> is like a war club, or a sword, or a sharp arrow.
> (Prov. 25:18)

Exaggeration

We also sin with our words whenever we exaggerate the truth. I'm not talking about embellishing as a literary device, times when story-telling is fun, and the audience knows the storyteller's colorful words are meant for effect. I'm talking about skewing the details of real life to garner attention. It may not seem like such a big deal, but over time all the words of an exaggerator lose credibility.

> The heart of the wise makes his speech judicious
> and adds persuasiveness to his lips. (Prov. 16:23)

Think about our natural response to television commercials. We don't really believe that Frosted Mini-Wheats will improve our kids' attentiveness by 20 percent, or that switching to Pantene Pro-V Moisture Renewal Shampoo will transform our genetically frizzy hair into silken strands. We don't believe it, because past experience has shown us that products routinely promise more than they deliver. Just so, if we routinely embellish the truth, people will begin to take all our words with a grain of salt.

It's something we must be on guard against, because we slip into it so easily. "I hate winter!" we say, but we probably don't, if we consider that hatred involves a strong, visceral desire for the destruction of someone or something. "My haircut is a total catastrophe!" Is it really? We might want to bounce that off a survivor of the 2011 Japanese tsunami. "I just adore cashmere!" Let's hope we don't, since to adore is to worship.

Exaggeration is the American way, but it is not the way of wise women, who know that, according to Jesus, they shall be held accountable for every careless word they utter.

Slander

Wise women avoid slander, which is the destroying of another's reputation. Proverbs tells us that slander is a trait of fools:

> The one who conceals hatred has lying lips,
>   and whoever utters slander is a fool. (Prov. 10:18)

Some years ago a young man in our community fell into some trouble and was placed under church discipline. Those of us who knew about it were warned by the church's pastor not to talk about the situation with outsiders in order to protect the young man's reputation. I was powerfully impacted by the pastor's instructions because from all accounts, the young man was clearly guilty of the wrongdoing. Nevertheless, discussing it could further have damaged him. Stories grow as they are told, and human nature being what it is defaults to believing the worst about someone. Because of that, we are capable of slandering someone even if what we say is factually right.

Careless Words

Another speech folly addressed in Proverbs concerns how much and when we talk. Proverbs links folly to a multitude of words—in other words, to talking too much:

> When words are many, transgression is not lacking,
>> but whoever restrains his lips is prudent. (Prov. 10:19)

We see there that restrained words are indicative of wisdom, which means that how much we talk is one way we are exposed to others as either foolish women or wise ones. Fools speak before they think, whereas the words of wise women are timely and well thought out. Wise women practice discernment with their words:

> Whoever restrains his words has knowledge,
>> and he who has a cool spirit is a man of understanding.
> Even a fool who keeps silent is considered wise;
>> when he closes his lips, he is deemed intelligent.
>> (Prov. 17:27–28)

> Do you see a man who is hasty in his words?
>> There is more hope for a fool than for him. (Prov. 29:20)

> The heart of the righteous ponders how to answer,
>> but the mouth of the wicked pours out evil things.
>> (Prov. 15:28)

> If one gives an answer before he hears,
>> it is his folly and shame. (Prov. 18:13)

Concerning that last verse, Proverbs 19:3, do we have a tendency to cut others off mid-sentence, assuming we know what they are going to say?

While we're on the subject, I can't help but think of those of us who walk through life with our cell phone affixed to our head as if it was an appendage of flesh. "I'm multitasking!" goes the explanation, but only in the last generation or two has multitasking come to be considered more virtuous than moments of silence and reflective thought. Besides, this is often an excuse we allow ourselves when, for whatever reason, we are ducking time alone with our thoughts. As I sat in cross-traffic last week, I decided to count the number of drivers I could spot talking on cell phones. Of the twelve cars that went by, there were eight cell-phone-using drivers; six of those were women. Phones on the road, in the dressing room, at the restaurant counter— we talk too much, and according to Proverbs there is folly in that.

In addition to the wisdom of when and how often we speak, there is even wisdom in the way we pitch our voice:

> Whoever blesses his neighbor with a loud voice,
>> rising early in the morning,
>> will be counted as cursing. (Prov. 27:14)

The immoral woman of Proverbs 7 is portrayed as having a loud voice:

> She is loud and wayward;
>> her feet do not stay at home. (Prov. 7:11)

And so is woman Folly:

> The woman Folly is loud;
>> she is seductive and knows nothing. (Prov. 9:13)

When it comes to how much and how often we talk and the voice we use to do so, here's wisdom:

> Whoever keeps his mouth and his tongue
>> keeps himself out of trouble. (Prov. 21:23)

Wise speaking not only keeps us out of trouble, but it also brings us joy:

> To make an apt answer is a joy to a man,
>> and a word in season, how good it is! (Prov. 15:23)

Gossip

One of the things Proverbs makes clear is how much our words affect our relationships. Gossip has a tremendous impact. We are told:

> A talebearer reveals secrets,
>> but he who is of a faithful spirit conceals a matter.
>> (Prov. 11:13 NKJV)

In other words, someone who gossips about another reveals an unfaithful spirit toward the relationship. Additionally:

> A dishonest man spreads strife,
>> And a whisperer separates close friends. (Prov. 16:28)

This proverb tells us that no matter how strong a foundation a relationship has, gossip can tear it apart. Think about your closest friendship: what bonds you? Isn't it your memories of shared experiences, both good and bad, and the confidences you've entrusted to each other as you work through life's complexities and hard times? Now consider what Proverbs teaches: gossip has the power to wipe all that out.

Although we know that gossip is sinful, we tend not to see it in quite the same destructive light that Proverbs does. We often view it as one of those "little" sins, something we know is wrong but not bad enough to wage war against in our hearts and lives. Some of us repackage the sin of gossip as "prayer concern," revealing personal tidbits about others' lives to our friends or Bible study group with hushed tones and concerned faces. Those of us who listen avidly are equal gossip participants. Do we realize that offering a receptive ear to gossip is as bad as voicing it?

Whether we listen to gossip or speak it, we are proving ourselves to be untrustworthy. So why do we do it? Sometimes we do it because we think it is a way to deepen a bond. "I'm really disturbed at what Sarah did last week," Sally tells Susie, "and I've just got to talk about it with someone. I'm telling you because I know I can trust you not to tell anyone." Ironically, Sally is undermining the very thing she wants from Susie—a deeper trust bond—because at some level, Susie realizes that if Sally can talk about Sarah to her, then Sally can just as easily talk about her to Sarah.

Gossip and all other speech sins stir up relational trouble. Think about every conflict you've ever had: wasn't it words of whatever sort that inflamed it? Probably right now we can all think of a conflict or two going on in our lives or among people we know. How can we use our words to respond to those conflicts wisely? One thing we can do is make a commitment not to involve ourselves in any gossip swirling around, whether by speaking it or listening to it.

> For lack of wood the fire goes out,
>> and where there is no whisperer, quarreling ceases.
>> (Prov. 26:20)

Since gossip has such negative consequences, why do we do it? As we already noted, one reason is that we believe the lie that it will bond us closer to those we gossip with. Another reason is this:

> The words of a whisperer are like delicious morsels;
>> they go down into the inner parts of the body.
>> (Prov. 18:8)

Primarily, Scripture says, we do it because it's enjoyable. The truth of this is proven by our response to the screaming headlines we see on supermarket tabloids—published gossip—while we are waiting in the checkout line. Just a passing glimpse at these headlines lets us in on the sordid affairs, legal troubles, addictions, and eating habits of the celebrities of the moment. A Christlike response would be sorrow, but instead we often feel good. The exposure of the travails of others makes us feel better about ourselves. "At least I don't have that trouble," we think with smug superiority, or, "My sin isn't as bad as hers." Peeking inside the private problems of those who are successful by the world's standards also makes us feel vindicated—all their money, perfect bodies, and Hollywood homes can't shield them from the same troubles that others have. We are reminded in black-and-white and four-color that worldliness doesn't pay what it promises.

Is this really so bad? It is, because we are renewing our satisfaction at others' expense. Consider how Asaph handled similar circumstances in his day:

> As for me, my feet had almost stumbled,
>   my steps had nearly slipped.
> For I was envious of the arrogant
>   when I saw the prosperity of the wicked.
> For they have no pangs until death;
>   their bodies are fat and sleek.
> They are not in trouble as others are;
>   they are not stricken like the rest of mankind. . . .
> Their eyes swell out through fatness;
>   their hearts overflow with follies.
> They scoff and speak with malice;
>   loftily they threaten oppression.
> They set their mouths against the heavens,
>   and their tongue struts through the earth. . . .
> Behold, these are the wicked;
>   always at ease, they increase in riches.
> All in vain have I kept my heart clean
>   and washed my hands in innocence. . . .
> If I had said, "I will speak thus,"
>   I would have betrayed the generation of your children.
> But when I thought how to understand this,
>   it seemed to me a wearisome task,
> until I went into the sanctuary of God;
>   then I discerned their end.
> Truly you set them in slippery places;
>   you make them fall to ruin.
> How they are destroyed in a moment,
>   swept away utterly by terrors! (Ps. 73:2–19)

Just as we do at times, Asaph wondered if following God's ways was worth it. As he looked at the worldly people around him, he saw their seeming advantages, and he was envious. But listening to gossip about the downfall of the worldly was not his path to peace. Rather, he found it by going into God's presence, which gave him long-range perspective. Additionally, it wasn't the downfall of the worldly that made him feel better; it was the fact that the purposes and glory of God and his ways will inevitably prevail, and therefore God's people can safely follow his ways.

Gossip makes us feel good, like eating tasty morsels, for a variety of reasons. Therefore, we are going to have to make every effort to resist it, perhaps lifelong effort. We are going to have to make a commitment not to "vent" or to spiritualize our words about others.

What about situations or relational conflicts in which we need advice or input from someone we trust? Surely there are times when discussing another person doesn't fall into the gossip category; in many of our relational conflicts we do benefit from outside help. When it comes to determining which is which in our particular case, usually our hearts will tip us off about why we want to talk about another, if we're honest enough to look. Are we seeking vindication? Are we bringing a third party into the conflict because we want someone to take our side? Or are we seeking help because reconciliation is what we're after? As with so many things, our motives make the difference.

Flattery

Another speech folly that Proverbs highlights is flattery:

> A lying tongue hates its victims,
>   and a flattering mouth works ruin. (Prov. 26:28)

Women steeped in biblical wisdom typically see right through flattery; they can sense the difference between a sincere compliment and flattering words. A compliment is offered as a means of building up, whereas flattery is spoken for personal gain. Complimenting is others-centered; flattering is self-centered. People who flatter are after something. Consider the stereotypical cad, a good-looking man with a slick tongue who woos a gullible and lonely woman out of her savings. How does he do it? He flatters her. She is the most beautiful creature to ever walk this earth, he says; and because she wants so desperately to be loved, she will do anything, even impoverish herself, to keep him around. His flattery has gotten him what he wanted.

Proverbs warns us to be careful and discerning:

> A man who flatters his neighbor
> spreads a net for his feet. (Prov. 29:5)

Flattery ensnares us where we are weak. It appeals to our desire to be loved, admired, and sought after. At some level, we all lust to be lusted after, and it is to this that flattery appeals. Flatterers are trying to get to us by appealing to this lust. Wise women not only guard their hearts from the flattering words of others, but they also guard their tongues from dishing out flattery of their own. We don't tell our boss that he delivered a fantastic speech at the board meeting, if his speech was mediocre. We don't tell the next-door neighbor that she is admired by everyone in town, just because we want an invitation to her next party. A modern slang term for flattery is "sucking up," which is what we are doing whenever we offer praise in hopes of personal profit.

transformed tongues

As we can see, how we use our tongues indicates in no small measure whether we are wise women or foolish ones. We will be known by what we say and how we say it. This truth is quite sobering, for who among us doesn't ever shade the truth or gossip or talk too much or flatter? We all sin with our words. It is at this point that we can see another way in which the book of Proverbs points us to Christ. We want to be wise, but as we discover that so much of what we say is actually foolish, we recognize that our need for wisdom far exceeds our ability to lay hold of it. A wise tongue comes only from the perfect Wise Man, who never spoke a foolish word. Jesus never lied, exaggerated, gossiped, or flattered. Every word he spoke was perfect for the occasion and accomplished God's purposes—every word. Only as we lean fully on him as the One who spoke perfectly for us will we find what we need to become women of wise words. And find it we will, if we look there. If we merely try harder to watch what we say, wise words will prove frustratingly elusive; we're just too sinful to ever master this on our own. Women of wise words are those whose hearts are being transformed by Christ while recognizing that real and lasting change comes only as they ponder all *his* words.

words of wisdom

It's worth the pursuit, and here's why:

> From the fruit of his mouth a man is satisfied with good,
> and the work of a man's hand comes back to him.
> (Prov. 12:14)

And

> The lips of the righteous feed many,
> but fools die for lack of sense. (Prov. 10:21)

Words governed by wisdom bless not only those who hear them but also those who utter them. Proverbs tells us explicitly how wise words bless and the ways in which wise women use them.

Soft Words

From Proverbs we learn that a certain tone of voice, a soft one, stops quarrels:

> A soft answer turns away wrath,
>> but a harsh word stirs up anger. (Prov. 15:1)

Soft words also bring healing:

> A gentle tongue is a tree of life,
>> but perverseness in it breaks the spirit. (Prov. 15:4)

We see again here that Scripture assigns value to our tone of voice. It matters more than we typically think, and recognizing this is a hallmark of wisdom.

Timely Words

A wise woman knows what to say and when to say it:

> The tongue of the wise uses knowledge rightly,
>> but the mouth of fools pours forth foolishness.
>> (Prov. 15:2 NKJV)

She knows when a rebuke is the best way to love someone:

> Better is open rebuke
>> than hidden love. (Prov. 27:5)

A wise woman also knows when to be quiet:

> Better is a dry morsel with quiet
>> than a house full of feasting with strife. (Prov. 17:1)

This even includes knowing when to share the things of God. Jesus told his followers, "Do not give dogs what is holy, and do not throw your pearls before pigs, lest they trample them underfoot and turn to attack you" (Matt. 7:6). Several years ago, I encountered the need for wisdom in this very context. Someone I cared about made sport of the Christian faith, and whenever I tried to communicate the gospel message, the response I received was cutting sarcasm and blasphemy. After one particularly painful exchange, the Holy Spirit brought Jesus's words in Matthew to bear on my heart, and from that day on for many years thereafter, I stopped mentioning anything about the Christian faith in her presence. I did not cease because my feelings were hurt; I stopped because Christ's name was being maligned, and I could sense the Spirit being grieved during those conversations. Years later, however, my friend was humbled by life's sorrows, and she became receptive to hearing the truth. I rejoiced as I began afresh to tell her about Jesus.

Knowing when to apply Jesus's mandate requires wisdom, because it is easy to mistake someone's reviling the gospel for what is really just our personal discomfort in talking about it to a skeptic. How, then, do we discern the difference? D. A. Carson helps us here:

> Jesus is commanding his disciples not to share the richest parts of spiritual truth with persons who are persistently vicious, irresponsible, and unappreciative. Just as the pearls were unappreciated by the savage animals, but only enraged them and made them dangerous, so also many of the riches of God's revelation are unappreciated by many people. And, painful as it is to see it, these rich truths may only serve to enrage them.[2]

ears of wisdom

Being a woman of wise words necessitates listening carefully to what others say. To that end, Proverbs teaches us the way to listen to a proven liar:

> Whoever hates disguises himself with his lips
>   and harbors deceit in his heart;
> when he speaks graciously, believe him not,
>   for there are seven abominations in his heart.
>   (Prov. 26:24–25)

This is powerful stuff. God's Word is warning us to be on guard against those who have knowingly lied to us in times past, and it is giving us a clue as to some of what resides within a liar's heart. While we cannot know others' hearts explicitly or accurately, God can, and graciously the Bible reveals a bit of that to us here. In light of this revelation and its call to be on our guard, we can echo those who say, "Lie to me once, shame on you. Lie to me twice, shame on me."

Another time that ears of wisdom are necessary is when we are trying to mediate a disagreement between others. Proverbs cautions us to listen to both sides before making a judgment about the matter:

> The one who states his case first seems right,
> until the other comes and examines him. (Prov. 18:17)

You know what they say: there are always three sides to every story—his, hers, and the real one.

How much better all our relationships will be—how much more peace we will have—when we become wise with our ears and our tongues! The apostle Paul wrote, "Let your speech always be gracious, seasoned with salt, so that you may know how you ought to answer each person" (Col. 4:6). Who is sufficient for these things? Only One: "The Lord God has given me the tongue of those who are taught, that I may know how to sustain with a word him who is weary" (Isa. 50:4).

the world . . .

"Even if a friend is saying the stupidest thing I've ever heard, I don't contradict her—because I wouldn't want her to be negative toward me."

—Charlotte, 34, *Marie Claire* magazine

the word . . .

Faithful are the wounds of a friend;
profuse are the kisses of an enemy.

—Proverbs 27:6

CHAPTER 4

wise women choose friends carefully

Commonalities make for friendships, my father told me when I was a teenager, and, being that I was at that painful age where friendships ebb and flow like ocean tides, his words had an immediate and profound impact. That very day, the social structure of high school suddenly made sense, and later I went on to see that the truth of his words isn't just about fleeting teen BFFs but about grown-up friendships too. We tend to bond with those whose lives intersect ours in one way or another. As we age, the nature of those intersections deepens. Bonding commonalities for teens—sports, grades, popularity—mature in adulthood (it is to be hoped) to those such as ethics and religious faith. Nevertheless, even as adults, many of the bonds we form spring from convenience rather than from conviction, from selfish motives rather than from godly ones.

Consider the friendships in your life. How did they come about? Was the bond formed thoughtfully or more by the shared commonalities of everyday life? Most of us have some of the latter—default friendships that arose originally from loose associations with our neighbors or coworkers and took root over time. Such friendships are important for gospel witness and the opportunities they present to exhibit the love of Christ, and also just because it's one of life's blessings to have rapport and camaraderie with those around us. Not every friendship needs to be formed only after lengthy consideration.

Some do, however, and those are the sort we are going to focus on in this chapter. By *friend*, we mean someone to whom we choose to entrust our hearts. We can rightly apply the word *friendship* to many of our relationships, but what we want to cover here are the sort we choose to let into our hearts and lives to the degree that they can significantly influence us. Friendships such as these need to be entered into carefully, as Proverbs makes clear:

> The righteous should choose his friends carefully,
>   For the way of the wicked leads them astray.
>   (Prov. 12:26 NKJV)

> Whoever walks with the wise becomes wise,
>   but the companion of fools will suffer harm.
>   (Prov. 13:20)

friendship pitfalls

Before we look at what Proverbs says about wise choices in friendship, let's step back and consider some obstacles that can steer us to foolish choices rather than wise ones. All things being equal, why do we choose to deepen the bond of certain associations but not others? Taking a look at what motivates us along these lines can prove helpful. Here are some of the pitfalls that reside in our hearts and lead us to make destructive friendship choices.

Sinful Desire

Years ago, while I was living in Center City Philadelphia, I resided across the alley from a heroin addict, a friendly but deeply lost young man. We chatted from time to time, and he would talk freely with me about his habit, just as if he were talking about a routine day at the office. There were certain business venues in the neighborhood—a video store and a corner pub—where daily he would walk up to the counter and purchase his drugs. I ate at that pub on one occasion, and because I knew what to look for, I witnessed at least a dozen of these illegal transactions during my meal. People from every walk of life—male and female, professional and prostitute—one by one entered the pub and made straight for a man, the drug dealer, perched on a stool at the end of the bar. A few words were usually exchanged between the dealer and his patron, and if you happened to glance down to just below the countertop, you'd see the exchange of money and a piece of folded yellow paper that contained a quantity of the illegal powder. Because of all that my neighbor shared with me in those across-the-alley conversations, I got a firsthand look at one aspect of the urban underground. I once asked my neighbor how drug users ferret out places such as the pub and the video store, and he said, "If you're looking for it, you're going to find it."

Friendships can form in much the same way. If we cherish some sinful indulgence or habit, our radar is going to be up for others who share our proclivity, and when we find someone who does, a bond can form almost instantly. Sometimes all it takes is a word or two. Maybe you know what I'm talking about. Take it from a heroin addict: if you're looking for it, you're going to find it.

Preventing such bonds from forming isn't ultimately about avoiding everyone who sins in areas where we struggle, although this may be necessary for a season. The only safeguard against the formation of this sort of destructive bond is to be radically honest with God about how much we love a particular sin, even though we know we should hate it. Real change begins not with trying harder not to do something sinful but with being truthful with God about the fact that we really don't want to try at all. Tell God, then tell a godly friend. Those are concrete steps on the road to repentance and to avoiding the snare of a destructive friendship.

a woman's wisdom

Ego Building

Pursuing friendships with those whose walk with God we respect is, according to Proverbs, a wise pursuit indeed. However, do we really yearn for a relationship with the Bible study leader, or do we simply want to be *known* for having a close association with her? Sometimes, it's not godly friendship we are after nearly so much as the reputation for being godly. Sadly, name dropping and social climbing happen in the church as much as anywhere else. Therefore, we do well to consider why and how we tell others that we had dinner with the pastor and his wife last week, or that one of the elders sought our husband's advice, or that we go walking every Tuesday with the local celebrity retreat speaker.

> Do not put yourself forward in the king's presence
> or stand in the place of the great,
> for it is better to be told, "Come up here,"
> than to be put lower in the presence of a noble.
> (Prov. 25:6–7)

The flipside of this is to be careful of our motives in deepening a relationship with someone who admires *us*. This is a very tempting thing to do when we are feeling particularly insecure or when we have recently experienced rejection. One way we can detect this motive in our hearts is if we find ourselves drawn to someone who flatters us. We already looked at what Proverbs teaches about flattery, and it cautions:

> Do not associate with one who flatters with his lips. (Prov. 20:19 NKJV)

Misplaced Identity

If we do not cling to Christ as our anchor, we are going to look for security somewhere—everywhere—else, most usually through our relationships. Sometimes, however unwittingly, we latch onto a friendship for the very purposes of filling that void in our hearts. Concerning this type of friendship, one thing is certain: it's not going to be harmonious for long. How can it be, when we are attempting to plug a human being into the place only God can fill? In such a friendship, each grasps at the other in some way in an attempt to get what each believes the other is required to give. Pop culture calls this "codependency." The Bible calls it "idolatry." Either way, God didn't design friendship as a means for selfish gratification. We are going to find ourselves dissatisfied with any relationship in which we are seeking to get more than we are seeking to give.

Of course, we all agree that friendships are a blessing to cherish rather than something to be used, but our hearts can trick us about our motives. Frequent turmoil in a particular friendship might serve as a call to examine our hearts.

Material Assets

Distasteful as it is to think about, Proverbs tells us that wealthy people are going to be liked by some just for their money:

> Wealth brings many new friends,
>   but a poor man is deserted by his friend. (Prov. 19:4)

And

> Many seek the favor of a generous man,
>   and everyone is a friend to a man who gives gifts.
>   (Prov. 19:6)

Some wealthy women recognize this unpalatable truth about human nature, and they use it to personal advantage, as a way to get friends. Others keep their guard up, shielding themselves from befriending anyone whom they suspect has a materialistic objective. A wealthy woman who fears the Lord, however, is able to acknowledge human nature while still loving those who seek her friendship, no matter their motives. While recognizing the limitations of such a friendship, she nevertheless won't get stuck on hurt feelings or cruelly reject someone who likes her for what she has rather than for who she is.

unwise friendship choices

It's not surprising that Proverbs is black-and-white about the wisdom of avoiding friendships with certain types of people. What is surprising are the actual types it warns about.

The Angry

Proverbs advises us not to make friends with angry people. Up until now, I don't think I have given the aspect of anger much thought when it comes to weighing the merits of my friendships. Have you? What does this mean, exactly? Does it mean we shouldn't befriend someone who can't control her temper, and if not, why not? In order to answer those questions, we need to remember that the focus here isn't day-to-day associations but rather those to whom we choose to give our hearts to the degree that we can be influenced by them. It is likely in that context that Proverbs cautions:

> Make no friendship with a man given to anger,
> > nor go with a wrathful man,
> lest you learn his ways
> > and entangle yourself in a snare. (Prov. 22:24–25)

The sort of anger in view here is not so much the occasional burst of verbal frustration at a recalcitrant child or an obnoxious driver. Rather, it is someone "given to anger," that is, someone characterized by an angry spirit. The concern expressed in the proverb isn't that we will begin to spew angry words but that we might find ourselves influenced by the thinking that underlies the heart of the angry one. A chronically angry person is generally not living by God's agenda. In fact, chronic anger indicates a heart at war with

God. Chronically angry people are those whose personal demands and expectations aren't being met, either by God or by those closest to them. A homemaker who bases her reputation on having a spotless home is going to be angry whenever she encounters clutter, muddy shoeprints, or unmade beds. Just so, a single woman who cannot accept her marital status might lash out in angry bitterness toward married women, whom she sees as more blessed.

We all have hopes and expectations, of course, but what is our heart's response when things don't work out the way we would like? A wise woman holds her hopes loosely and trusts that if they do not materialize, God knows best. Chronic anger, on the other hand, is the typical response of those with a my-way-or-the-highway mindset. It is pure pride, and that's what Proverbs is warning us about. Close association with the proud, whose pride is revealed by their chronic anger, is always a danger to our hearts, because we are all proud by default. Living close to Christ is the only way to keep pride from regaining its mastery.

The Self-Indulgent

Another important thing to consider in a prospective friend is her level of interest in and her commitment to sensual enjoyments. In other words, we are wise not to choose as our closest companions those who are fixated on earthly, fleshly pleasures. A good rule of thumb by which we can measure our spiritual health in relation to created things is *indifference*. Can we take or leave certain food and drink, or having our nails done, or that vacation in Aruba? Our freedom to enjoy such things extends only as far as our not needing them. God has given us all things to enjoy, as Paul wrote (1 Tim. 6:17), but Proverbs warns:

> Be not among drunkards
>   or among gluttonous eaters of meat,

for the drunkard and the glutton will come to poverty,
and slumber will clothe them with rags. (Prov. 23:20–21)

On the other hand, we know that Jesus spent time with serious partiers (Matt. 11:19; Luke 7:34). So what are we to conclude when we have these passages before us that seem to guide us into polarized courses of action? This is where we see so clearly the need for the wisdom that comes from God's Word. Wise women—those who govern their lives by the fear of the Lord—are discerning women. They have learned to take into account not only what Scripture says about a particular topic but also the big picture of Scripture, before determining how to apply it. In choosing whether to deepen a friendship with a woman who seems overly given to sensual enjoyment, a wise woman will consider the fact that people are free to enjoy all God has given in creation, but she will balance that by also considering what Scripture says about the consequences of overindulgence. She will recognize that Jesus did indeed spend time with heavy drinkers, but she will see that his purpose in doing so wasn't worldly; it was redemptive. As a result of studying Scripture, she might then conclude, for the sake of her own spiritual well-being, that deepening the friendship is unwise, but she can commit to an association that includes regular gospel witness.

In this and every factor we consider when determining the depth of a particular friendship, we remember the truth of what someone has wisely observed: "We are conformed to that upon which we center our interest and love." And more weighty still are Paul's words: "Do not be deceived: 'Bad company ruins good morals'"(1 Cor. 15:33).

how to choose

So how do wise women go about choosing their friends? In other words, how do they determine those to whom it is wise to entrust their hearts? Proverbs shows us what to look for:

As iron sharpens iron,
So a man sharpens the countenance of his friend.
(Prov. 27:17 NKJV)

The primary criterion for choosing a friend is whether the relationship, overall, brings us closer to the Lord. Hopefully, as you consider the proverb, you can readily identify a friend or two who fits the description. I don't mean that you do nothing but read Scripture and talk about spiritual things when you get together. I mean, rather, that after you have spent time together, your view of God is bigger and more joy filled, and you find yourself motivated to know God better. Of course, in such a friendship there will naturally be much conversation about spiritual things, as well as open accountability about struggles with sin; but even after lighthearted get-togethers—a day at the zoo or a trip to the mall—when nothing of great depth is discussed, you find your heart filled with gratitude *to God* for the friendship.

A simple question to ask ourselves about the nature of a particular relationship is this: Does it cause me to flourish or diminish, both as a woman made in the image of God and in my walk of faith? If the relationship is a wise one, both people will be edified spiritually.

A wise woman isn't afraid to befriend those who speak up about sin. In fact, she gravitates toward such friendships because those who are honest about sin—their own and their friends'—tend to care more about what God thinks than about being popular.

Oil and perfume make the heart glad,
and the sweetness of a friend comes from his earnest
counsel. (Prov. 27:9)

In his day, Jeremiah cried out against those who made light of sin, those who minimized how much God hates it as well as the consequences of it. Concerning such people, God spoke through the prophet, saying, "They have healed the wound of my people lightly, saying, 'Peace, peace,' when there is no peace" (Jer. 6:14). Do we want friends who will hold us accountable for what we do? If so, we won't get overly close to those who wink at our questionable practices and say, "That's no big deal." Which type are we drawn most toward? We might be quick to point to the first type, but the truthfulness of our answer is most accurately revealed by where and with whom we are spending our time. The bottom line is that our choices in friendship are only ever a reflection of where we are—or where we are seeking to be—with the Lord. If our relationship with God is primary, we are going to choose friends who strengthen that, and we will, therefore, recognize the truth of this:

> Faithful are the wounds of a friend;
>   profuse are the kisses of an enemy. (Prov. 27:6)

Not only in Proverbs but throughout all of Scripture we find instruction and wisdom for how to go about choosing our closest companions. The apostle Paul wrote this: "I appeal to you, brothers, to watch out for those who cause divisions and create obstacles contrary to the doctrine that you have been taught; avoid them" (Rom. 16:17). Paul was writing here about people who cause trouble in the church and stir up controversy between believers.

Paul also gave explicit instructions to avoid close ties with Christians whose lifestyles deny their professions of faith:

> I wrote to you . . . not to associate with sexually immoral people—not at all meaning the sexually immoral of this world, or the greedy and swindlers, or idolaters, since then you would need to go out of the world. But now I am writing to you not to associate with anyone who bears the name of brother if he is guilty of sexual immorality or greed, or is an idolater, reviler, drunkard, or swindler—not even to eat with such a one. (1 Cor. 5:9–11)

Not only are we to avoid an intimate friendship with believers who live in unrepentant sin, but we are not even to associate with them.

This is hard to put into practice, because it just feels so judgmental. But it's actually an act of love—love for God and for the one caught in sin. First, it's an act of love toward God because we are refusing to wink at what dishonors him. Second, we are demonstrating to the practicing sinner that sin is serious. Avoiding such a one not only serves to guard our own hearts from temptation and to uphold God's honor, but it can also serve to convict the heart of the sinning one.

Some years ago, a man I knew, a professing Christian, came out and admitted his lifelong struggle with homosexual temptation. Edward had tried for years to deny his temptation, but he'd gotten tired of the struggle and had decided to quit the battle. My heart aches for Edward, because he never learned the rest and peace that comes from leaning on Christ. He walked out on his wife and kids, and today he lives openly with a male partner. He is also actively involved in an organization that promotes homosexuality as a biblically acceptable lifestyle. While this is, of course, deeply troubling, it is also troubling that a number of Edward's former church friends continue the friendship as if nothing had changed and embrace the two men as a couple. These friends know God's Word; so either they are blatantly disregarding what Paul said to do in such cases, or they are ducking it because upholding it would prove painfully uncomfortable. According to Paul, if Edward's friends really loved him, and if they took God's Word seriously, they would kindly and gently put him out of their fellowship after explaining why.

We must, of course, balance Paul's words in Corinthians with what he wrote to the Galatians: "Brothers, if anyone is caught in any transgression, you who are spiritual should restore him in a spirit of gentleness. Keep watch on yourself, lest you too be tempted" (Gal. 6:1). Notice the difference in wording between the two passages. There is a difference between being caught in a transgression and living a lifestyle of unrepentant sin. A fruit of wisdom is discernment, which means that, in cases such as these, wise women have a feel for which biblical instruction is best applied in a particular case. There are times—probably more often than not—when cutting a sinning believer out of our fellowship would be the wrong application. Is our sinning friend miserable about her sin and desiring to overcome it, even though she slips up again and again? If so, the Galatians passage is one we do well to study and apply with our friend. One the other hand, if she is defensive and argumentative about her sin and insisting on her own way over a long period of time, we might consider talking to our pastor about if and how the Corinthians application might be appropriate. If we suspect that this is the most loving approach, we do well to seek advice and get the help of a pastor or another mature believer. In either case, a commitment to love must be the goal—love for our friend, love for God, and love for our own spiritual safety—and wise women prayerfully evaluate the depth of the friendship accordingly.

Friend or Rescuer?

Proverbs issues this caution:

> My son, if you have put up security for your neighbor,
>   have given your pledge for a stranger,
> if you are snared in the words of your mouth,
>   caught in the words of your mouth,
> then do this, my son, and save yourself,
>   for you have come into the hand of your neighbor:
>   go, hasten, and plead urgently with your neighbor.
> Give your eyes no sleep
>   and your eyelids no slumber;
> save yourself like a gazelle from the hand of the hunter,
>   like a bird from the hand of the fowler. (Prov. 6:1–5)

What is Proverbs 6:1–5 about? We know it doesn't mean that we shouldn't step up and help people in trouble, because all through Scripture we are admonished to do just that. So, then, what do these words mean, and how are we to apply them?

Basically, the passage is about not taking on responsibility that belongs to another. Conversely, of course, mercy does just that. We see in the New Testament epistle Philemon that Paul assumed the debt belonging to the runaway slave Onesimus. Above all, Jesus took on and paid our sin debt by dying on the cross. But wise women are able to distinguish between showing mercy and assuming misplaced identity. Sometimes taking on someone else's responsibility is harmful. Notice the language of the passage: *snared, caught, save yourself from the hand of the hunter.* The language implies that there are people who prey on the kindness, weakness, or assets of others, and that when a wise woman realizes she has fallen into such a relational tangle, she will get herself out of it.

An application of the passage can be made to the sort of relationship that psychologists today label "codependent." Proverbs calls it "the fear of man":

> The fear of man lays a snare,
> but whoever trusts in the LORD is safe. (Prov. 29:25)

Whatever term you use, it is applicable to relationships in which two people seek to find meaning, identity, or escape from life's troubles in what they can get from or do for the other. The Bible, however, says that seeking meaning and identity in anything or anyone apart from Christ is idolatry. And idolatry always leads to slavery, the language of which we see in Proverbs 6:1–5. If we are undiscerning about such relationships in our own lives or about our individual temptations to relational idolatry, we might find ourselves ensnared.

Disentangling from the snare of this sort of relationship is easier said than done. Relational idolatry occurs when people are made so big in our hearts that God is made small, and once that has happened, pleasing a person becomes much more important to us than pleasing God. Ed Welch explains:

> I have spoken with hundreds of people who end up at this same
> place: they are fairly sure that God loves them, but they also want

or *need* love from other people—or at least they need *something* from other people. As a result, they are in bondage, controlled by others and feeling empty. They are controlled by whoever or whatever they believe can give them what they think they need. It *is* true: what or who you need will control you.[1]

The way out is found only through looking away from the relationship and toward God. While we are still caught up in the snare of idolatry, this can seem impossibly hard to do, which is why James Boice asks:

> What will cure us of the idols of our lives? Not another idol certainly. Not will power, for we are dead in trespasses and sins and therefore have no will at all in spiritual matters. The only thing that will do it is a vision of Him whose glory eclipses all else and whose love draws us to Himself alone.[2]

We will see that restoring God to his rightful place in our affections enables us to love him supremely, and it also brings us clarity about how to love another. We will see that our efforts to rescue our friend and to control her problems have actually hindered her from turning to God. Looking away from the relationship involves an act of repentance. It includes reorienting our thinking. It involves acknowledging that we have been ensnared by our sin. And sometimes it will mean obliterating the relationship from our lives. The biblical remedy for idolatry is always destruction of the idol, not massaging or manipulating it.

The prophet Hosea shows the steps on the path out of idolatrous relationships and the blessings that come after we have repented:

> Return, O Israel, to the LORD your God,
>   for you have stumbled because of your iniquity.
> Take with you words
>   and return to the LORD;
> say to him,

"Take away all iniquity. . . .
We will say no more, 'Our God,'
to the work of our hands. . . ."

And afterward this is what God will do:

I will heal their apostasy;
   I will love them freely,
      for my anger has turned from them. . . .
They shall return and dwell beneath my shadow;
   they shall flourish like the grain. . . .
O Ephraim, what have I to do with idols?
   It is I who answer and look after you.
I am like an evergreen cypress;
   from me comes your fruit. (Hos. 14:1–8)

Our friendships must be chosen with an eye to what most pleases God, not ourselves or another. We do this by keeping biblically based love principles in mind—whether it's our time, our money, or our lives that we are offering to someone.

being a friend

We've considered how the Bible guides us in choosing our friends. But that's only half the equation. How can we *be* a good friend? We can begin here:

A friend loves at all times,
   and a brother is born for adversity. (Prov. 17:17)

There we see that deciding against entering into or continuing a close relationship with someone is not the same as a refusal to love. Sometimes love requires disassociation, as we just considered.

On another, less weighty note, Proverbs gives this piece of practical advice on being a good friend:

a woman's wisdom

> Let your foot be seldom in your neighbor's house,
>> lest he have his fill of you and hate you. (Prov. 25:17)

In other words, good friends don't overstay their welcome. A practical way to love others is to be cognizant of their needs and the value of their calling and their time. Do friends duck our calls because they can never get us off the phone? Do they not invite us to drop by for mid-morning coffee because we might stay through lunch?

The wisdom of keeping our foot from being too often in our neighbor's house can also be applied to the place we seek to hold in her affections. In other words, a possessive spirit will hinder us from being a good friend. We aren't to treat our friendships as personal possessions. If we find ourselves jealous of the time a friend spends with others or distressed when she reveals confidences to someone besides us, we aren't acting with her best interests in mind.

Being a good friend also means knowing when to mind our own business:

> Whoever meddles in a quarrel not his own
>> is like one who takes a passing dog by the ears.
>> (Prov. 26:17)

There is always risk when we involve ourselves in the relational difficulties of others, yet sometimes we take the risk because it's the loving thing to do. When we are asked to get involved by mediating an argument or offering advice, we do so, knowing full well that our involvement might come back to bite us. However, if we offer our two cents unsolicited, we might rightly be accused of meddling. Just because we believe that our third-party objectivity will provide insight that those directly involved in the difficulty are unable to see, it doesn't mean our input is necessary. It takes discernment—and humility—to determine when to speak up and when to keep quiet. That being said, it is always right to seek the best way to confront blatant and unrepentant sin. Apart from that, however, it is often wisest simply to make ourselves available to help rather than to step up and try to assert it.

At the same time, wise women don't look away when their friends are caught up in sin, nor do they gloss over the sin when asked about it as we consider again a proverb we looked at earlier:

> Faithful are the wounds of a friend;
>> profuse are the kisses of an enemy. (Prov. 27:6)

When a friend asks if we've noticed her recent thirty-pound weight gain, we tell her the truth. We use her question as an opportunity to dig deeper, perhaps asking if there is an underlying struggle that she has been using food to cope with. Our bluntness may wound her initially, but it will help her much more than saying, "What thirty pounds? I don't know what you're talking about!" when it is clear that we do indeed. Or when we've noticed that a particular friend has been acting a little too friendly with her married colleague, pointing it out is the act of a faithful friend. Ignoring it because it's awkward or because we fear she will think we are legalistic is more like the kiss of an enemy.

the ultimate friend

So many of those we call "friends" pass through our lives in a season or two. What bonded us in the first place—those areas in which our lives intersect—changes over time, and then the relational glue no longer holds. Or one of us grows spiritually while the other does not. Friends will let us down, and we will let them down too. I've heard it said that if we get to old age with two or three friendships that have survived all of life's changes, we should consider ourselves rich in friends. Jesus, however, is the ultimate friend and the only one who will never let us down. And this is a friendship that all wise women embrace. "No longer do I call you servants, for the servant does not know what his master is doing; but I have called you friends, for all that I have heard from my Father I have made known to you" (John 15:15).

Morgan - Job opport.
 - ticket accident done
 - Mom Mst Visit

April -

Lydia - husband praise
 - calm his heart

Diane - hives
 - Cold
 - hlth Ins praise
 - daughter decisions
 Bethany

Jessica - Court
 - Job
 - Guidance
 - Grandparents moving

Bonnie - Sister visiting
 < Court
 - financial
 - husband hlth

the world . . .

"Don't let yourself come last! It's important for you to be able
to indulge in things that are just for 'you.' You deserve it!"

—Jennifer LB Leese,

"Indulge Yourself! 20 Fantastic Ways to Feel Fantastic,"

The Woman's Connection

the word . . .

It is not good to eat much honey,
nor is it glorious to seek one's own glory.

—Proverbs 25:27

CHaPTeR 5

wise women know the secret of self-control

When you think of self-control, or the need for it, what probably comes to mind, if you're an American, is eating. We live in a society that has more opportunity to indulge personal appetites than any society throughout history. And indulge we do, to the point that we don't know how to stop. Our grocery stores provide us with hundreds of food choices, and some restaurant menus take as long to peruse as the latest issue of *Bon Appétit*. The Food Network features multiple how-to programs and cooking competitions, and good chefs today possess celebrity status.

Don't get me wrong—I greatly enjoy watching many of these programs. But I can't help but cringe sometimes at the disproportionate value placed on how something looks or tastes. Table settings are no longer discussed in terms of placemats and candles; today they are *tablescapes*. And just listen to what *Top Chef* judge Gail Simmons had to say about a contestant's sauce: "That pepperoni sauce was just crazy. . . . It was intense! It was really intense. . . . It made us think, it was thoughtful and focused, and somehow it came together. It cracked me up."[1] Pepperoni has become so much more than just a tasty pizza topping; today it is thoughtful, focused, and amusing.

Some time ago, actor George Clooney was interviewed on television. He had lost a lot of weight for a movie role, and the reporter asked, "George, what is your diet secret?" And he replied, "I don't eat too much." It was apparent that the reporter didn't quite know how to respond to his simplistic weight-loss strategy, so she changed the subject, but George unwittingly spoke some biblical truth:

> If you have found honey, eat only enough for you,
>   lest you have your fill of it and vomit it. (Prov. 25:16)

That proverb speaks much-needed wisdom into our food-saturated culture.

Have you felt the extremes of overeating—not just the physical ones but the emotional "vomiting" that occurs after overdoing it? We always feel lousy afterward because we are filled with regret and self-recrimination. Despite those bad feelings, we tend to downplay the sin aspect of overeating. We soften it and refer to last night's "overindulgence" and in more extreme cases to someone's "eating disorder." But no matter what we call it, the Bible calls it gluttony:

> Be not among drunkards
>   or among gluttonous eaters of meat,
> for the drunkard and the glutton will come to poverty,
>   and slumber will clothe them with rags. (Prov. 23:20–21)

We are gluttonous whenever we eat more than we need, whatever the underlying motivation. We are gluttonous whenever we misuse God's good gift of food to gratify ourselves or to escape troubling emotions or to seek control over life. That's why those with the eating disorder anorexia also fall into the glutton category. Anyone who has ever misused food as a way to cope with stress, alleviate boredom, or escape loneliness knows the truth of this proverb:

One who is full loathes honey,
>   but to one who is hungry, everything is sweet.
>   (Prov. 27:7).

In America today, eating, for many, is all about pleasure, but in many places around the globe, food is still more about basic survival. Eating disorders and other outworkings of gluttony aren't prevalent in underdeveloped countries, but the abundance of food in the West has made it an easy avenue for the outworking of our sin. We take food for granted and misuse it rather than eating for the purpose of glorifying God with good health and with thankfulness for his bounty. Proverbs gives us a rule of thumb for eating biblically:

> It is not good to eat much honey,
>   nor is it glorious to seek one's own glory. (Prov. 25:27)

In other words, eating in moderation is good. It enables us not only to glorify God but also to enjoy our bounty of food as God intended.

what exactly is self-control?

How would you define self-control? The first thing we might say is that self-control is something difficult. We know this from personal experience. We might define it this way: self-control is getting—and maintaining—a grip on ourselves, which includes a grip on our emotions, our speech, and all our physical appetites. Wise women recognize that mastering the art of self-control comes from submitting to *God's* control in every area of life. To be self-controlled, therefore, is actually to be controlled by God.

Self-control is also something we all *need*, and Proverbs tells us why:

> A man without self-control
>   is like a city broken into and left without walls.
>   (Prov. 25:28)

Ancient cities were surrounded by impregnable walls. These walls served as the front lines of defense against would-be attackers. We read in the book of Joshua that the Israelites were not able to get inside the city of Jericho until God miraculously caused the walls of the city to come tumbling down (Josh. 6:15–20). Understanding this aspect of ancient cities enables us to grasp the metaphor in the proverb. Without the walls of self-control, we have little defense against our enemies, which consist of anything that weakens or diminishes our ability to obey God and glorify him with our lives.

Paul teaches us something about self-control in his letter to the Galatians. In chapter 5 of that letter he makes a contrast between being led by our natural desires and being led by the Holy Spirit. He indicates the contrast by providing us with two lists. The first is a list of things, "works of the flesh," that spring from our fallen nature, and the second is a list of traits, the "fruit of the Spirit," that will be manifested in us as we are progressively mastered by Christ. The works of the flesh aren't hard to pinpoint, as he says:

> The works of the flesh *are evident*: sexual immorality, impurity, sensuality, idolatry, sorcery, enmity, strife, jealousy, fits of anger, rivalries, dissensions, divisions, envy, drunkenness, orgies, and things like these. I warn you, as I warned you before, that those who do such things will not inherit the kingdom of God. (Gal. 5:19–21)

In other words, certain habits and behaviors are shown to be sin by the negative fruit they produce, the ultimate outcome of which is separation from God and his kingdom. Every item on that list is an outworking of sin. Each has a controlling, addictive quality that, if left unchecked, will eventually take over and master a life.

Elsewhere Paul provides us with a spiritual perspective on this downward spiral. Using sexual perversion as an example, he gives us insight into the heart-working of those who are enslaved by what today we call "addiction":

Claiming to be wise, they became fools, and exchanged the glory
of the immortal God for images resembling mortal man and
birds and animals and creeping things. Therefore God gave them
up in the lusts of their hearts to impurity, to the dishonoring of
their bodies among themselves, because they exchanged the truth
about God for a lie and worshiped and served the creature rather
than the Creator, who is blessed forever! Amen. For this reason
God gave them up to dishonorable passions. (Rom. 1:22–26)

Proverbs puts it this way:

> The iniquities of the wicked ensnare him,
>   and he is held fast in the cords of his sin.
> He dies for lack of discipline,
>   and because of his great folly he is led astray.
>   (Prov. 5:22–23)

When people seek fulfillment apart from God himself, they initially think they are on the path to delight and freedom, but the reality is just the opposite. They are fools, because they are looking to
gratify their cravings in what God has created rather than in the One
who created them. Over time, God gives them up to their cravings. If
you read that entire chapter of Romans, you will see that being given
over to the sinful desires of our flesh is God's ultimate judgment on
unrepentant sin.

Some time ago I ran into an old acquaintance whom I hadn't
seen in twenty years. As we caught up over coffee, he told me that
since I'd seen him last, he'd spent many years away from the Lord
and gotten caught up in unrestrained sexual sin. He was seeking the
Lord afresh, he said, but he continued to struggle with desire for
some of the perverted practices in which he'd engaged. As he told
me a bit of this, he said with a wry smile, "I did some pretty awful
things, and I'm surprised that God didn't strike me down in the process." He didn't realize that his desire for perversion was itself a fore-
taste of what eventually would have happened in full measure had

he not repented. Such is the nature of sin and God's dealings with it, whether we are Christians or not. James Boice writes:

> When we are sliding downhill we delude ourselves into thinking that we are only going to dip into sin a little bit or at least that there are points beyond which we will never go, lines we will never cross. But this is sheer fantasy. When we start down that downhill path, there are no points beyond which we will not go and no lines we will not choose to cross—if we live long enough. . . . When we come to Christ, the question is not "How low can you go?" We are done with that. The question is "How high can you rise?" And to that question the answer also is: no limit. We are to become increasingly like the Lord Jesus Christ throughout eternity.[2]

And this is right where Paul's second list fits in: "But the fruit of the Spirit is love, joy, peace, patience, kindness, goodness, faithfulness, gentleness, self-control; against such things there is no law" (Gal. 5:22–23).

Here we discover that the self-control of Proverbs 25:28 isn't a natural trait, something that, if we just try hard enough, we can master. Our understanding of it is much fuller as a result of what we find in Galatians. In both Testaments, it is clear that self-control is possible only by and through the living Lord. In Proverbs we know it as the fear of the Lord, living under him in trust, submission, and dependence. In the New Testament we get a much fuller picture. Self-control comes about through our union with Christ. Only those who live in fellowship with God can apprehend and maintain true self-control. Any of us can modify our behavior, but behavior modification is not the same thing as self-control, because, from a biblical standpoint, only one of those—self-control—has to do with the whole person—body, mind, and heart.

Who doesn't want this? We all want to be characterized by self-control. But how? How can we live this way on a consistent basis?

We all can relate to Paul, who said, "I do not understand my own actions. For I do not do what I want, but I do the very thing I hate" (Rom. 7:15). We would all prefer to be in control rather than to be controlled by something or someone, yet each of us struggles with how to lay hold of it in one or more areas of our lives. But God never leaves us in the dark where obedience is concerned:

> Walk by the Spirit, and you will not gratify the desires of the flesh. For the desires of the flesh are against the Spirit, and the desires of the Spirit are against the flesh, for these are opposed to each other, to keep you from doing the things you want to do. (Gal. 5:16–17)

And

> Those who belong to Christ Jesus have crucified the flesh with its passions and desires. If we live by the Spirit, let us also keep in step with the Spirit. (Gal. 5:24–25)

Paul shows us that when it comes to getting hold of and maintaining self-control, there is a balance between what God does and what we do. As for our part, we are to walk by the Spirit and crucify our flesh; in other words, we are to starve the life out of the natural urges that threaten to master us, and we are to walk by the Spirit, which means presenting ourselves regularly to God's Word and other believers so that, in the process, we will be transformed into the image of Christ. Paul was stating a fact when he said that if we walk by the Spirit, we won't constantly succumb to things that harm us. If we are in Christ, we can be self-controlled women.

This is good news. If we have experienced repeated failure in our attempts to quit overeating, overspending, or whatever our particular struggle might be, *it doesn't have to be this way*! But so often it still is. Too often we find ourselves like the broken-down city left without walls. What tears down our walls? Let's consider five possibilities.

five hindrances to self-control

1) Competing Desires

One reason we struggle is that our desire for control is constantly at war with our desire for the thing we need control over. If you are a woman whose weight fluctuates like a yo-yo, you know what I'm talking about. Every winter you gain ten pounds, and every summer you take off eight. Over time, you resolve to lose those cumulative extras, and you do, only to find the scale climbing back up a few months later. Either you will eventually become discouraged and simply give up, or you will continue to yo-yo for the rest of your life. *But it doesn't have to be this way!*

Whether the issue is weight or something else, yo-yoing with any behavior is a tip-off that we are in the midst of an internal war. We have a love-hate relationship with a thing or a desire or a substance. We don't want to be ruled by this thing, but at some level we don't want to give it up either. We don't like the negative effect it is having on us—our bodies, our relationships, our spiritual walk—but at some level, in some way, we are getting a pay-off from indulging in it. A woman who stress-eats hates the outcome—she gains weight, her clothes are tight. At the same time, she doesn't want to give up the escape from stress that food provides her. She cannot master self-control over her eating because her desire to lose weight competes with her desire for the instant, if short-lived, stress relief that she experiences while eating. Jesus said, "Every kingdom divided against itself is laid waste, and no city or house divided against itself will stand" (Matt. 12:25). If we are torn between two desires, we won't get anywhere.

2) Wrong Motives

Sometimes self-control remains elusive because we seek it for the wrong reasons. If we have been asking God to help us cultivate self-control in a particular area, yet we don't seem to be making progress, perhaps God is answering in a way we haven't considered. He might be directing us to examine our hearts. Why are we praying for self-control? If it's solely because we are sick and tired of the consequences of our overindulgence, or because we want to feel better about ourselves, we are leaving God out of the equation. God isn't interested in helping us with our self-improvement program; he is interested in our holiness. James wrote, "You desire and do not have, so you murder. You covet and cannot obtain, so you fight and quarrel. You do not have, because you do not ask. You ask and do not receive, because you ask wrongly, to spend it on your passions" (James 4:2–3).

Self-improvement doesn't necessarily bring us closer to God or glorify Christ. It usually has more to do with self-glory. Holiness, on the other hand, enables closer fellowship with God and brings glory to him, and a by-product of personal holiness is the very thing we were looking for in the first place—general well-being and freedom from the destructive effects of sin. We will find self-control much easier to come by if we desire it because we want to remove obstacles in the way of our relationship with God.

Besides, self-improvement attempts that aren't motivated by love for God aren't likely to be successful in the long run. In his parable about an unclean spirit, Jesus was painting a scary picture of what happens to those who attempt to earn their own righteousness, but it can also apply to those who try to manage their lives in any way apart from a vital relationship with God. When the unclean spirit returns to its place, it finds the house swept clean and put in order. "Then it goes and brings with it seven other spirits more evil than itself, and they enter and dwell there, and the last state of that person is worse than the first" (Matt. 12:43–45).

3) Underestimating the Destructive Power of Overindulgence

Something beneficial in the beginning will destroy us in the end if we do not exercise self-control over it. But all too often we don't look far enough down the road. We overindulge because we crave immediate satisfaction. There are lots of things that provide an immediate fix—an escape from stress, boredom, or loneliness—but using God's good gifts in creation as anesthesia for life's difficulties doesn't work for very long. Before we know it, we realize that we've been tricked. What started out as an enjoyable diversion has become something we don't know how to live without. "Whatever overcomes a person, to that he is enslaved," wrote the apostle Peter (2 Pet. 2:19), and Proverbs tell us:

> There is a way that seems right to a man,
>   but its end is the way to death. (Prov. 14:12)

Alcoholics and drug addicts never intended to become enslaved. In fact, it's safe to say that they assumed they never would. Discussing such things in a book for Christian women is not misplaced, because Christians are not exempt from the ever-growing population of those caught in these snares. And just consider how much the Bible—written to and for God's people—has to say about the dangers of alcohol abuse. No, Christians are not exempt. I recently heard someone joke, "The difference between Presbyterians and Baptists isn't drinking or not drinking; it's that Presbyterians drink in the open, and Baptists drink in secret." I was saddened by her cynicism, especially because she was a relative newcomer to the faith, and this is what she had observed in her short tenure in the church of Jesus Christ.

There is always a demonic component to substance abuse. Drugs and alcohol numb the conscience, quashing the inherent restraint to sin that our conscience affords us. That's why people do all sorts of horrendous things under the influence of drugs and alcohol, things that their consciences would otherwise hold in check. Many a fall into sexual sin is fueled by alcohol, as are relational disagreements, rash spending, and hastily uttered words. Additionally, the abuse of drugs and alcohol leads to personal and relational destruction—the Devil's goal for everyone. All sin destroys, but there is something about substance abuse that reveals this so clearly. Proverbs paints a picture of how alcohol destroys:

> Who has woe? Who has sorrow?
>> Who has strife? Who has complaining?
> Who has wounds without cause?
>> Who has redness of eyes?
> Those who tarry long over wine;
>> those who go to try mixed wine.
> Do not look at wine when it is red,
>> when it sparkles in the cup
>> and goes down smoothly.
> In the end it bites like a serpent
>> and stings like an adder.
> Your eyes will see strange things,
>> and your heart utter perverse things.
> You will be like one who lies down in the midst of the sea,
>> like one who lies on the top of a mast.
> "They struck me," you will say, "but I was not hurt;
>> they beat me, but I did not feel it.
> When shall I awake?
>> I must have another drink." (Prov. 23:29–35)

We want to think that Christians are less susceptible to the enslavement of alcohol or drugs, but if that were true, Paul wouldn't have found the need to instruct, "Older women . . . are to be reverent in behavior, not slanderers or slaves to much wine" (Titus 2:3). There he was speaking specifically of Christian women. We also must not kid ourselves that overindulgence is only about having too much at any one time. It can also be about imbibing *too often*. If you enjoy wine with your dinner, can you take it or leave it? Indifference is key. We are free to enjoy something only to the degree that it doesn't matter to us one way or the other.

John Piper doesn't drink, but he is clear that Scripture doesn't prohibit the consumption of alcohol. He gives four basic reasons why he chooses not to imbibe: (1) his conscience won't let him, and he knows that while drinking may not be sinful, violating one's conscience is (Rom. 14:22–23); (2) alcohol is a mind-altering drug; (3) alcohol is addictive; and (4) he wants to make a social statement. About this last one he writes:

> I choose to oppose the carnage of alcohol abuse by boycotting the product. If people can go on hunger strikes to make a political statement, and boycott Nestle's products to make a statement about child nutrition and third world exploitation; if people can go without lettuce for the sake of solidarity with Southern Californian farm workers, or swear off white bread and granulated sugar, is it really so prudish or narrow to renounce a highway killer, a home destroyer, and a business wrecker?[3]

We all know that alcoholism in our society is rampant indeed, whether or not we handle it the way John Piper does—with total abstinence. If we relish our biblical freedom to enjoy a drink, we are only free to the degree that we can take it or leave it. Therefore, if we find that we are unable to deny ourselves an indulgence—alcohol, or food, or television, or spending, or romance—and refuse to face that fact and deal with it, we will eventually experience the truth of this:

> Whoever loves pleasure will be a poor man;
>   he who loves wine and oil will not be rich. (Prov. 21:17)

4) Failure to Know Ourselves

Are you savvy about the things that trip you up, those particular temptations that suck you into the pit of sin again and again? Sometimes we don't know because we don't want to know. But this refusal is the kiss of death where self-control is concerned. It is also pride. Women who grow strong in self-control are those who humbly acknowledge their particular weaknesses. Only the humble can recognize and admit to their weaknesses, and it is this same humility that finds grace to repent of self-sufficiency and lean on Christ for the routine practice of self-control. Paul said, "Let anyone who thinks that he stands take heed lest he fall" (1 Cor. 10:12).

Sometimes, however, rather than acknowledge sin and temptation, we point instead to our "addictive personality." But that's a weak argument. We've all got an addictive personality to one degree or another because we are all sinners in whom the "desires of the flesh" clamor to be fulfilled. Knowing where we are weak is crucial in the battle for holiness because only then will we develop an effective strategy against it. Such self-awareness is also a vital component of wisdom.

Wise women learn to recognize their personal triggers. Does boredom compel you toward food? Does stress drive you to drink or to painkillers? Does loneliness suck you into hours of repetitive and mindless television? Does sorrow drive you out the door to the mall? Whatever it is, name it for the God-substitute it is and commit to turning from it.

5) We Think That Self-Control Should Be Easy

Another reason that self-control remains elusive is that we think it should be easy because we are Christians. A motto in Alcoholics Anonymous is "Let go and let God," but the slogan is theologically inaccurate. "Wait a minute," some argue. "Aren't we supposed to depend on God for everything?" We are indeed. And one of the things we depend on him for is the personal exercise of self-control. All too often we are looking for effortlessness, not strength. The strength God gives is the enabling to overcome, but the enabling will likely require vigorous work, all the same. Paul wrote, "For this I toil, struggling with all his energy that he powerfully works within me" (Col. 1:29). He also wrote, "Work out your own salvation with fear and trembling, for it is God who works in you, both to will and to work for his good pleasure" (Phil. 2:12–13). And we saw in Galatians that we are to crucify the flesh, which is not exactly the picture of a quick and painless death. We also saw in Galatians how we are to go about it: "Walk by the Spirit, and you will not gratify the desires of the flesh" (5:16). That is the theologically accurate slogan. The AA version leaves out Christ, and it is only in him that we have the Spirit to walk by.

Christ is key

The fruit of the Spirit, which comes out in us through our union with Christ, includes self-control. So, if we are in Christ, we have all we need to be self-controlled women. Concerning the fruit of the Spirit, one characteristic of which is self-control (Gal. 5:23), Don Matzat writes:

> Our "religious" focus is not to be directed at spiritual gifts and blessings but at the person of Jesus Christ. If we desire the forgiveness of sins and a righteousness that is acceptable to God, *God gives us Jesus*. If we seek peace, joy, and love, *God gives us Jesus*. If we desire comfort in the midst of sorrow, hope when things look hopeless, assurance when plagued by doubt, and contentment through the changing scenes of life, *God gives us Jesus*. All spiritual gifts are simply manifestations of the new life of Christ dwelling with us, manifested spontaneously as we walk in the Spirit by directing our consciousness unto Jesus.[4]

All told, there are four factors that give wise women their self-control. First, they live for something greater than themselves—Christ—and as a result, they desire to be like him. Those who live for Christ find that he is what makes life worth living.

Second, wise women depend on Christ in order to be made like Christ. They live out Jesus's words: "Abide in me, and I in you. As the branch cannot bear fruit by itself, unless it abides in the vine, neither can you, unless you abide in me" (John 15:4). Third, wise women apply themselves to putting sin to death with sustained effort. Fourth, they pray for a spirit of moderation, as we see modeled in Proverbs:

> Remove far from me falsehood and lying;
> > give me neither poverty nor riches;
> > feed me with the food that is needful for me,
> lest I be full and deny you
> > and say, "Who is the LORD?"
> or lest I be poor and steal
> > and profane the name of my God. (Prov. 30:8–9)

God in Christ wills that our walls be strong and fortified against our triad of enemies: the world, the flesh, and the Devil. *Yes, it can be this way*!

the world . . .

"It's sort of cheesy, but having a *que sera, sera* sort of outlook has pulled me through a lot—and I've always come out chipper on the other side."

—Maridel Reyes, *Glamour* magazine

the word . . .

Desire without knowledge is not good,
and whoever makes haste with his feet misses his way.

—Proverbs 19:2

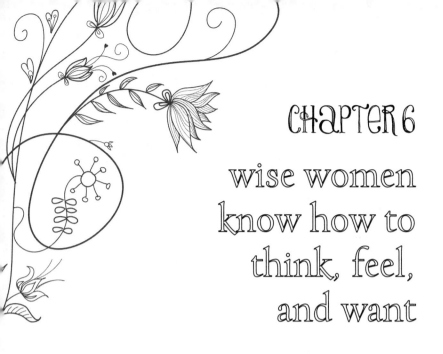

CHAPTER 6

wise women know how to think, feel, and want

There are three things about us that significantly shape the course of our lives: what we think, what we feel, and what we want. The way in which we handle our thoughts, our feelings, and our desires determines not only our path but whether that path is joyful and fulfilling or fraught with discontentment.

God created us as thinking and feeling creatures, and therefore both are part of being made in his image. That is why both thoughts and feelings are vital components of true faith. A grasp of God and the gospel that is solely intellectual is barren of the relational joys that God desires us to have with him. On the other hand, if our faith is informed primarily by who we *feel* God is rather than by careful study of Scripture, we are going to wind up with an inaccurate picture of his character. That being said, it is clear from Scripture overall that feelings are meant to be subservient to thoughts rather than the reverse.

Women, more so than men, I think, are prone to be ruled by

feelings, perhaps because our emotions tend to be close to the surface. It is much rarer to see a man burst into tears of frustration in the midst of a bad day. Because we are wired as emotional beings, women who are wise nourish and tend their thought life as carefully as a gardener tends her rose bushes, so that her feelings don't get the upper hand and so that her desires are formed around biblical principles.

thinking

Proverbs makes a connection between righteous living and careful thinking:

> A wicked man puts on a bold face,
> But the upright gives thought to his ways. (Prov. 21:29)

Also made clear is that harmful naiveté is overcome by using our minds:

> The simple believes everything,
> but the prudent gives thought to his steps. (Prov. 14:15)

However, later in the book is another proverb concerning our thought life that seems to contradict everything we've just looked at:

> Whoever trusts in his own mind is a fool,
> but he who walks in wisdom will be delivered.
> (Prov. 28:26)

Is Solomon claiming here that too much thinking is unwise? He is not. His point has to do with humility. Thinking is wise, and giving careful thought to our ways is godly, but relying on our thoughts as authoritative is foolish. In other words, while we are to use our minds in all we do and plan, we are to submit all those thoughts and actions and plans to the lordship of Christ, which is the way to "walk in wisdom." Doing so is often a struggle, however, because even as believers we are so prone to self-reliance. We all naturally want to be in charge of our own lives, and because that's the case, we miss the contrast Solomon makes here. Either we can trust in our own mind or we can walk in wisdom. Those two options are mutually exclusive.

A well-developed mind can also breed popularity and success:

> A man is commended according to his good sense,
>   but one of twisted mind is despised. (Prov. 12:8)

The irony is that, as we taste the fruit of careful thinking (that life just works better!), we might find ourselves tempted, consciously or not, to rely less on God and more on ourselves. We avoid this danger by understanding that our minds are meant to be servants of God rather than servants of our personal happiness, as Paul wrote: "I appeal to you therefore, brothers, by the mercies of God, to present your bodies as a living sacrifice, holy and acceptable to God, which is your spiritual worship. Do not be conformed to this world, but be transformed by the renewal of your mind, that by testing you may discern what is the will of God, what is good and acceptable and perfect" (Rom. 12:1–2).

A wise woman pursues single-mindedness, which means she seeks to make her chief aim in life the glory and enjoyment of God. A foolish woman, on the other hand, is double-minded and content to stay that way. To women such as this, James has strong words: "Draw near to God, and he will draw near to you. Cleanse your hands, you sinners, and purify your hearts, you double-minded" (James 4:8). The word James used means "two-souled"; in other words, to be double-minded is to be split in two directions. A double-minded woman lives consistently divided in her thoughts, affections, and desires between competing loyalties, unlike the single-minded woman, who runs after one goal, one ambition, and one overarching desire.

a woman's wisdom

Wise women may not yet have arrived at single-mindedness, but they want it, and they go after it, and they take James's instructions to heart by actively seeking to cleanse their hands (what they do) and to purify their hearts (what they think and feel and want). There are things in each of us that dilute our heart purity. What is it for you? Well, one way to know is to consider what rules your thoughts when you lie awake in the middle of the night, or where you go in your mind when you crave a quick-fix mental escape from stress, or what tends to obsess you.

We think of an obsession as a fixation on a desirable outcome or object, but there is something spiritually dark about obsession. It can be a foothold for the Devil. Obsessive thoughts are those that hook us; we can get caught on them and find ourselves unable to let go, even when we want to. Although we often can't recognize the root of the problem, we can be sure that underlying obsessive thinking is an out-of-control desire to master something or someone, which springs from doubts about God's mastery of the situation or even doubts about God himself. Writing about obsession in its full-blown state, what is labeled "obsessive-compulsive disorder," Michael Emlet writes:

> Obsessions are "persistent ideas, thoughts, impulses, or images that are experienced as intrusive and inappropriate that cause marked anxiety or distress." More simply put, obsessions are "sticky thoughts"—thoughts that individuals can't seem to get out of their minds. . . . OCD sufferers want to live in a black-and-white world. Exhaustive knowledge, complete control, and being certain allow no room for ambiguity. Either I'm sure or I'm not; either I'm in control or I'm not; either I'm right or I'm not. Yet we must admit we live in a "gray" world: God reveals enough knowledge to live sanely before Him, but He doesn't give us full access to His mind (cf. Job 38–41). God gives us the ability to choose freely and to act, but we are not able to know and master all the details of our world. God gives us direction in His Word, but many issues are not so clear-cut. This shows the importance

of the biblical category of wisdom. It's "safer" to live in a black-and-white world, because it requires no trust! Trust and wisdom go hand in hand.[1]

Wise women guard their minds from obsessive thoughts by trusting God and his sovereign control at all times over all circumstances.

Thinking Intelligently about Thinking

Back in the 1970s the United Negro College Fund adopted as their slogan a quote from Malcolm X: "A mind is a terrible thing to waste." For much of each day our minds are occupied with the tasks that make up our God-given callings, but in those few daily or weekly hours of downtime, what do we choose to read and watch and listen to? It's all too easy to assume that something with a certain label—a Christian song, a G-rated movie—is pleasing to God, but to rely on labels that have been assigned by the culture at large, or even by other Christians, as the means for such assurance is a bit of a cop-out. It requires no thought on our part. And the fact is that much of what passes as clean entertainment today is just trivial or inane.

God, through the apostle Paul, has provided us with a rating system for our entertainment choices that far exceeds that assigned by the Motion Picture Association of America: "Whatever is true, whatever is honorable, whatever is just, whatever is pure, whatever is lovely, whatever is commendable, if there is any excellence, if there is anything worthy of praise, think about these things" (Phil. 4:8).

This tells us that God is glorified by excellence. Therefore, we are more in keeping with Paul's teaching if we fill our ears with a secular piece of music beautifully composed than with a poorly crafted contemporary praise song with trivial lyrics. Just so with literature and films. James Boice writes:

> According to this verse the Christian is to decide between doubtful things by choosing the best. This does not exclude the best

things in our society, whether explicitly Christian or not. For the meat of the verse lies in the fact (not always noticed by Bible teachers) that the virtues mentioned here are pagan virtues. . . . On the whole they are taken from Greek ethics and from the writings of the Greek philosophers. In using them, Paul is actually sanctifying, as it were, the generally accepted virtues of pagan morality. . . . The things that are acknowledged to be honorable by the best people everywhere are also worthy to be cultivated by Christians. Consequently, Christians can love all that is true, noble, right, pure, lovely, and admirable, wherever they find it.[2]

Therefore, Paul's command actually broadens rather than narrows the scope of what we as Christian women are free to enjoy as we seek to please God. But it takes thought. There is a mental investment required to determine whether that particular book or movie or television program we are considering fits Paul's criteria. Wise women exercise discernment in deciding what will occupy their thoughts. And this aspect of wisdom is not too hard, because "God has not given us a spirit of fear, but of power and of love and of a sound mind" (2 Tim. 1:7 NKJV).

The Blessings of Thinking Biblically

There are particular blessings enjoyed by women who practice wise thinking. To the woman who sets her mind on God comes unruffled peace: "You keep him in perfect peace whose mind is stayed on you, because he trusts in you" (Isa. 26:3). Added to peace is the promise of real living: "To set the mind on the Spirit is life and peace" (Rom. 8:6).

There is also the promise, found in a verse we considered earlier, that as we present our minds to God's Word for transformation, we will discover that God's ways with us are wonderful: "Be transformed by the renewal of your mind, that by testing you may discern what is the will of God, what is good and acceptable and perfect" (Rom. 12:2). Again we are helped in our understanding by James Boice:

> When Paul encourages us to prove that God's will is a pleasing will, he obviously means pleasing to us. That is, if we determine to walk in God's way, refusing to be conformed to the world and being transformed instead by the renewing of our minds, we will not have to fear that at the end of our lives we will look back and be dissatisfied or bitter, judging our lives to have been an utter waste. On the contrary, we will look back and conclude that our lives were well lived and be satisfied with them.[3]

feelings

Just consider the roller-coaster ride of emotions we can experience in the course of a single week (or, for some of us, a single day): anger, love, frustration, joy, sorrow, annoyance, irritation, fear, anxiety, peace, satisfaction, exultation, discouragement, happiness, fulfillment, dissatisfaction, anticipation. The list could go on. I've met some even-keeled women over the years, and I used to chalk it up to natural-born temperament. Over time, however, I've come to see that such equilibrium has as much to do with maturity as it does with birth.

We are quick to blame our circumstances or our hormones for our mood swings, and there is no doubt that the stresses of life and body do have a significant impact on how we feel. Nevertheless, we don't have to be—nor should we allow ourselves to be—victimized by our feelings. The wild fluctuation of our hormones at certain times may challenge our tolerance of others or depress our outlook, but nowhere does the Bible give us a hormonal pass on the call to kindness, patience, contentment, joy, and love. Instead of being victimized by what provokes negative emotions, we can view the provocations the way Paul viewed his thorn in the flesh. If God doesn't remove the thorn as a result of our pleading, we have an opportunity to experience Christ's sufficiency in the midst of it.

Of course, none of us is ever going to master our emotions completely. For one thing, God didn't create us to be robots. He designed us to feel the ups and the downs. Additionally, it is often the down times and our wrestlings in them that produce the most spiritual fruit. Therefore, wise women don't debunk their feelings; rather, they take charge of them. Elisabeth Elliot advises:

> Do not try to fortify yourself against emotions. Recognize them; name them, if that helps; and then lay them open before the Lord for His training of your responses. The discipline of emotions is the training of responses.[4]

This "training of responses" is how wisdom is lived out and how we become characterized as women of wisdom. We're going to consider how to handle our emotions wisely by looking at two particular emotions—anger and grief—and in doing so, we'll get an idea of how the wisdom of Proverbs can be harnessed for the whole spectrum of our emotions.

Anger

Some anger is good. After all, Jesus got angry with those who abused temple practices for greedy gain (Matt. 21:12–13). But we are not Jesus. I once heard a wise pastor say that this side of glory we will never experience fully righteous anger. We just aren't capable of it, since everything about us is sin-tainted. But that doesn't mean that all the anger we experience is wrong or that we should never get angry. After all, Paul wrote, "Be angry and do not sin; do not let the sun go down on your anger" (Eph. 4:26), and Brian Chapell writes:

> There are just causes for righteous anger. Injustice, cruelty, and insensitivity to others stir God's wrath and rightly cause anger in us who are made in his image. . . . Christians sometimes cripple their own emotional health and progress in relationships by refraining from expressing the cause of tensions under the false

presumption that all anger is wrong. We can properly, directly, and biblically experience anger (Mark 3:5; Matt. 18:34). The apostle does not forbid anger but the sinful expression of it.[5]

A woman seeking to grow in wisdom is increasingly able to live out Paul's instruction, and Proverbs provides us with a way to do so. We learn from Proverbs that anger governed by wisdom includes self-restraint:

> Whoever is slow to anger has great understanding,
> but he who has a hasty temper exalts folly. (Prov. 14:29)

> Whoever is slow to anger is better than the mighty,
> and he who rules his spirit than he who takes a city.
> (Prov. 16:32)

In fact, when it comes to anger management, being "slow to anger" is advised repeatedly in Proverbs (10:11; 14:29; 15:18; 16:32), more so than any other approach to this powerful emotion.

Elsewhere Solomon wrote, "Be not quick in your spirit to become angry, for anger lodges in the heart of fools" (Eccles. 7:9). Here he not only reinforces what he wrote in Proverbs, but he adds this piece about anger that festers. This is the sort of anger that gets stuck in our hearts. We can't stop thinking about it; we toss and turn at night, rehearsing the cause of our anger over and over in our minds. We can't stop talking about it; we vent our rage to others, or we post it in an anonymous comment in all capital letters on a blog. Anger that is easily come by and that takes up residence in our hearts indicates the presence of folly (sin). It is being angry *with* sin rather than angry *without* sin.

Getting a handle on our angry emotions can be very difficult, especially when our anger seems justified. So how do we do it? Proverbs does provide us with some concrete steps, but, even more importantly, it reveals an overarching principle: we don't become wise by employing anger management techniques—even those provided in Proverbs. Managing our anger isn't something we do; it's something we become. It's actually the fruit of wisdom.

> Good sense *makes* one slow to anger,
>> and it is his glory to overlook an offense. (Prov. 19:11)

We also see there that overlooking a wrong—giving it a free pass and simply letting it go—is commendable, such as when your spouse or friend or colleague said something insensitive to you or misjudged your motive or gave credit to someone else for something that you did. Isn't it true that most of our anger comes from feeling slighted, disrespected, or not given our due? How often do we get our hackles up because Jesus has been slighted, disrespected, and not given *his* due? Chances are that there is disproportion there in all our hearts.

Of course, there are times when overlooking an offense is a cop-out. Confrontation is unpleasant, and often we fear its outcome. But when God's name is dishonored, or when a Christian persists in unrepentant sin, or when someone demonstrates repeated disregard for the welfare of others, overlooking the offense might be more foolish than wise for all involved.

Grief

Another emotion that we find very difficult to manage is grief. When we are in the midst of a season of sorrow, there are times when crushing feelings of grief just rise up seemingly out of the blue and overtake us. Certainly there is nothing unwise about grief—it's just part of being human, as Proverbs says:

> A glad heart makes a cheerful face,
>> but by sorrow of heart the spirit is crushed. (Prov. 15:13)

Precisely because grief crushes the spirit, we and those around us profit when we learn how to handle it biblically. First, we ought to note that Proverbs does not engage in personal grief counseling. Its approach is more about cultivating in us an awareness of the feelings of others. We can say, therefore, that, according to Proverbs, wise women are intuitive about others' pain.

In terms of handling our own grief, we can learn a good bit about that from King David. There came a point in David's reign when his son Absalom turned on him and sought to kill him in order to obtain David's throne for himself. He gathered a band of renegades and sought to carry out terrorist attacks against his father the king and the royal army. Can you imagine the hurt David felt? His own child wanted him dead. Wealthy parents probably taste a bit of what David felt if, as they age, their children express little interest in their well-being but a lot about what's in their will.

For a season, David's life was in danger, but in the long run, Absalom's gang was no match for the king, who sent his army to stop the uprising led by his son. As the army prepared to head into battle, David issued this request: "Deal gently for my sake with the young man Absalom" (2 Sam. 18:5). We see there a father's heart: no matter that his son wanted to kill him, David wanted his son's life spared. But that's not how it worked out. The army had no compunction about slaying Absalom; they had the welfare of the entire kingdom to think about, not just the king's feelings. Absalom was killed in the battle, and when word reached David that his son was dead, he cried, "O my son Absalom, my son, my son Absalom! Would I had died instead of you, O Absalom, my son, my son!" (2 Sam. 18:33).

Despite Absalom's betrayal, David was overcome with grief when he received word of his son's death. If you are a parent, surely you can resonate with David's response. We all can, for that matter, because the death of a loved one, even when (perhaps especially when) the relationship has been fractured before the death, is heartbreaking. The presence of powerful emotions such as grief is not a matter of wisdom or the lack thereof; but how we handle those emotions has everything to do with it. David's response discouraged those who had risked their lives for him:

> The victory that day was turned into mourning for all the people, for the people heard that day, "The king is grieving for his son." And the people stole into the city that day as people steal in who are ashamed when they flee in battle. (2 Sam. 19:2–3)

As word of David's grief spread dishearteningly throughout the city, David's advisor Joab came and rebuked the king:

> You have today covered with shame the faces of all your servants, who have this day saved your life and the lives of your sons and your daughters and the lives of your wives and your concubines, because you love those who hate you and hate those who love you. For you have made it clear today that commanders and servants are nothing to you, for today I know that if Absalom were alive and all of us were dead today, then you would be pleased. (2 Sam. 19: 5–6)

Joab's words penetrated David's grief, and he got himself together for the sake of his people. Nevertheless, we have in David an example of emotions run amok. Both his love for his son and his grief at his death were poorly contained, and his failure to "rule his spirit" (Prov. 16:32) had rippling consequences. Arthur Pink writes, "The excessive indulgence of any passion (grief by no means excepted), not only offends God, but betrays men into great imprudences in their temporal concerns."[6]

Therefore . . .

Considering all this in light of Proverbs' emphasis on being in tune with the feelings of others, we can summarize the wisdom of emotional restraint as "giving free reign to emotions only to the extent that doing so brings no harm to people or dishonor to God's name."

desires

Our desires—the things we want—tend to govern our lives and our choices. For that reason, it is important that our desires get formed in a biblical mold. Right now, today, we all desire something. It might be a desire we've carried in our heart for years, or perhaps it's more recent. It might be something that springs from our feminine nature—a husband, a child, a home of our own. Some of us desire healing, either for an illness or for a relationship. It might be a desire for a major change, such as a different job or a relocation. It could be something simpler such as a break in the routine by means of two weeks at the beach or just by getting out of the kitchen for a night or two. It is to be hoped that above all our desires, we desire God himself.

Sometimes the way in which we describe a particular desire is merely our attempt to give shape to some deeper yearning in our hearts that we cannot name. Our desire for marriage, home, and family, for example, may be how we give expression to our longing for love, belonging, and the banishment of loneliness. No matter the specifics of our desires or how we express them, all our longings are indicative of the fact that we aren't home yet. We are unfinished women living in an unfinished world, and because of that, we aren't going to find full satisfaction until we get home, until we are perfected in Christ and living with him in heaven. Until then, we are going to remain women who want.

Many of the things we desire are hardwired into us. God designed us to want home and family and to be fed and clothed and sheltered; and there is nothing wrong with these desires. The problem is that we tend to want them too much. When that happens, good desires get warped into slave masters. We are enslaved to any desire that we believe we must have in order to be content. For that reason, we do well to consider what Proverbs says about our desires.

Proverbs distinguishes between good desire and bad, and

between good, better, and best, and it puts wisdom at the forefront of desirable acquisitions.

> Wisdom is better than jewels,
>> and all that you may desire cannot compare with her.
>> (Prov. 8:11)

What the Word of God is telling us here is that no matter how worthwhile our desires, nothing will prove as rewarding and satisfying as the obtainment of wisdom. Since this is true, you'd think we would set our passions to work on laying hold of it much more than we do. If we craved wisdom as much as we do things and relationships and success, we'd be much more contented than we often are. It is God's will to provide us with wisdom, whereas it may not be in his plan to give us any number of the other things on which we set our hearts, which is what accounts for most discontentment.

In fact, it might actually be that God withholds something we want because our desire for it is so intense that having it would prove harmful to us. David Powlison says, "Our desires for good things seize the throne, becoming idols that replace the King. God refuses to serve our instinctive longings, but commands us to be ruled by other longings. What God commands, He provides the power to accomplish."[7] So the first thing we learn about desires from Proverbs is that the best desire—and the one we are guaranteed to get—is wisdom.

Proverbs does indeed indicate that when our desires are aligned with God's truth, we can be much more confident about his providing them:

> What the wicked dreads will come upon him,
>> but the desire of the righteous will be granted.
>> (Prov. 10:24)

> The desire of the righteous ends only in good;
>> the expectation of the wicked in wrath. (Prov. 11:23)

The psalmist said it this way: "Delight yourself in the LORD, and he will give you the desires of your heart" (Ps. 37:4).

Proverbs is also tuned into the *power* of desires:

> Hope deferred makes the heart sick,
>   but a desire fulfilled is a tree of life. (Prov. 13:12)

> A desire fulfilled is sweet to the soul,
>   but to turn away from evil is an abomination to fools.
>   (Prov. 13:19)

Consider the contrast in that last proverb (13:19). It is likely that, at some point, all of us have tasted the sweetness of a dream come true. Fools, however, taste sweetness in giving themselves to sin. But it is a temporary fulfillment at best and never sweet for long.

Proverbs also gives us insight into what happens when we allow our desires to rule our lives:

> Whoever isolates himself seeks his own desire;
>   he breaks out against all sound judgment. (Prov. 18:1)

Described here is someone who is so set on pursuing what she desires that she won't listen to others' advice or guidance. Over time, she begins to avoid anyone who might challenge her pursuit of what she wants, and eventually she is likely to find that those naysayers were right all along. We see this proverb played out every day, often in ungodly romantic entanglements.

When it comes to something we desire, Proverbs is saying, we handle it wisely by welcoming the input of others in order to guard ourselves against the power of want. That bit of wisdom is reinforced here:

> Desire without knowledge is not good,
>   and whoever makes haste with his feet misses his way.
>   (Prov. 19:2)

a woman's wisdom

Proverbs also makes clear that we, as fallen creatures, will experience desires for sinful things or for too much of a good thing, and that there are consequences for giving in to them:

> The desire of the sluggard kills him,
>> for his hands refuse to labor. (Prov. 21:25)

The sluggard, for example, has an inordinate desire to experience comfort and pleasure without having to work for it. Our mental image of a sluggard is someone who sleeps till noon, then lounges on the recliner all day with the clicker in hand and a bowl of chips nearby. But the couch potatoes aren't the only sluggards; physically active people can be sluggards too.

Bethany, an unemployed twenty-eight-year-old, wants a job, and since she has been unemployed for over a year, she desperately needs one. But Bethany isn't willing to take just any job; no, she wants a dream job. Bethany has been encouraged by friends and family to apply for positions that in time could lead her to a dream job, but Bethany doesn't like that suggestion and is unwilling to consider it.

When I went to college to study communications, I was blessed to attend what was considered a top-notch communications school. Despite the school's reputation, I'll never forget what one professor told the class—and I'm dating myself here—near the end of our senior year: "Don't think you're going to graduate from this school and step into a plumb job in journalism or publishing or television. No, if you want to break into it, you women will start as secretaries and you men will begin in sales." He was talking about due paying. And he was right. Bethany doesn't want to pay dues, nor does she think she should have to, because she is attractive and has a college degree. If we seek to build our lives on a foundation of entitlement, we are living as sluggards. Humility, which goes hand in hand with wisdom, recognizes and accepts that due paying is part of life.

If our desires are shaped by the fear of the Lord, we will find them coming true: God "fulfills the desire of those who fear him" (Ps. 145:19). Additionally, those who fear the Lord are those who desire the Lord. The psalmist not only knew this, but he lived and breathed it: "Whom have I in heaven but you? And there is nothing on earth that I desire besides you" (Ps. 73:25). If we want to taste the joy of fulfilled desire, this is the way. If our desire is for God himself, we are guaranteed to get him in Christ. And the more of him we know and experience, our desires for lesser things will diminish proportionately, because nothing is more fulfilling than God in Christ. Have you tasted this? If so, you know exactly what the psalmist was talking about. If not, are you willing to pray that God would make this your ruling desire? If you are, you are guaranteed the joy of desire fulfilled.

> Blessed is the one who finds wisdom,
>   and the one who gets understanding,
> for the gain from her is better than gain from silver
>   and her profit better than gold.
> She is more precious than jewels,
>   and nothing you desire can compare with her.
>   (Prov. 3:13–15)

the world . . .

"Some people feel that they don't deserve to be wealthy or that there is only so much of the millionaire pie to go around. Creating wealth and financial freedom is available to everyone. It is our right to be wealthy, and my hope is that people take their space and know they deserve it."

—Loral Langmeier, "8 Myths About Money,"
—*The Millionaire Maker*

the word . . .

A rich man's wealth is his strong city,
and like a high wall in his imagination.

—Proverbs 18:11

CHAPTER 7

wise women are financially savvy

"I have no idea what our financial situation is," Natalie said. "My husband takes care of all that, and I'm so glad, because thinking about bills and taxes and retirement savings is beyond me." Of course it's beyond her—she has invested no time or thought in learning about it. And while husbands manage the money in many if not most households, there is tremendous wisdom in getting a handle on the state of our family finances and knowing where the records are kept and who the contacts are. If a wife unexpectedly loses her husband, the devastation, both emotionally and practically, will be intensified if she does not know or understand the state of her financial affairs. Conversely, wives who discipline themselves to keep abreast of the family finances not only fare better if left suddenly alone but can also be more actively supportive while their husband is still with them.

We find such a wife in Proverbs 31 (a woman we are going to look at in-depth later on). The wife of Proverbs 31:11–31 is a picture of wisdom. She was placed at the end of the book to serve as an illustration of what a young man should look for when choosing a spouse. A quality for which she is commended is her financial know-how. She devoted time to discovering a good investment opportunity, and she grew her investment so that it was profitable (Prov. 31:16). She also understood the value of the commercial goods of her day and used that knowledge to generate income (Prov. 31:18, 24).

From her we learn that it is biblically right for a wife to be financially shrewd. Too often today, in our well-meaning efforts to control the damage done by the feminist movement to God's design for marriage, we go too far in the opposite direction. In our desire to uphold male leadership in our home, we steer clear of things like finances, but this is the wrong way to go about it. We can actually help our husband more if we know what's going on with our bank accounts, because we can serve as well-informed sounding boards and offer intelligent input into financial decisions rather than leaving him isolated in having to deal with it all alone.

Whether married or single, we are called to contribute to the financial well-being of our household. The contribution of a married woman may be either direct or indirect, whereas for a single woman it is most often direct. In addition to acquiring knowledge about how to save and invest, a single woman must also earn the money in order to do so. In either case, the principles of financial wisdom are the same. First, Proverbs makes a direct link between prosperity and hard work, laziness and poverty:

> A slack hand causes poverty,
>> but the hand of the diligent makes rich. (Prov. 10:4)

> In all toil there is profit,
>> but mere talk tends only to poverty. (Prov. 14:23)

> Whoever works his land will have plenty of bread,
>> but he who follows worthless pursuits will have plenty
>> of poverty. (Prov. 28:19)

Proverbs 14:23 is a verse for Bethany, whom we saw in the last chapter. It shows us that we are blessed by undertaking even the most mundane tasks, whether the blessing comes immediately or down the road. Concerning finances, the verse applies to our efforts to *earn* as well as our efforts to *learn*. Elsewhere Solomon wrote, "In the morning sow your seed, and at evening withhold not your hand, for you do not know which will prosper, this or that, or whether both alike will be good" (Eccles. 11:6).

the power of the purse string

Proverbs also gives us wisdom about borrowing money, making clear that there are always, if often invisible, strings attached:

> The rich rules over the poor,
>   and the borrower is the slave of the lender. (Prov. 22:7)

While sometimes unavoidable, indebting ourselves to a person or an institution is always risky business. There are times when borrowing makes good long-term sense for ourselves and our family's well-being. After all, very few can plunk down the asking price for a house or even a car. But if we default on repayment of the debt, we are in worse shape than we were before we undertook it, and to avoid the consequences—the slavery Proverbs speaks of—it is wise to discern, so far as we can today, whether the amount we are borrowing is manageable. Counting the cost in advance of any undertaking is wise, as Jesus made clear when he asked, "For which of you, desiring to build a tower, does not first sit down and count the cost, whether he has enough to complete it?" (Luke 14:28).

But let's get beyond the Suze Orman basics. Our lives can become enslaved to a lender in much more subtle ways. If we take that loan from our husband's parents, are we going to feel obligated to spend every holiday with them for the next decade? If we encourage our husband to accept financial help from our own father, is he going to feel the need to defer to our dad concerning things unrelated to the loan, perhaps breeding resentment in the process? It is always wise to weigh the long-range slavery potential any time we are thinking of borrowing money.

Some time ago, my friend Leisel borrowed money interest-free from a family member for college tuition, which has proven to be a tremendous blessing. However, she paid off the loan as soon as she could, because she felt guilty every time she spent a dollar on a nonnecessity. Her lender never raised an eyebrow or questioned her spending, and he would have felt bad if he'd known how the loan has made her feel; nevertheless, she was enslaved to the lender. Sometimes borrowing is indeed unavoidable, but other times, if we would simply separate out real need from want, we'd see that we could avoid the danger spelled out in Proverbs 22:7.

the weight of wealth and the power of God

Even money we've acquired through our own diligence can be a hassle:

> The ransom of a man's life is his wealth,
> but a poor man hears no threat. (Prov. 13:8)

The more you have, the more can be taken from you and the more there is to worry about. We drive along those tree-lined streets with houses set far back from the road, and we admire—and perhaps envy—the manicured lawns, and we envision the beauty of the home's interior and furnishings. But do we stop to consider the upkeep of such a lawn? It represents either the effort of a father-and-son team every summer Saturday or the regular work of an expensive yard service. As for what's inside, all that silver needs polishing—and insuring. High ceilings need professional painters, and high-priced upholstery needs special cleaning. The more you have, the more you spend. "Nevertheless," we say, "I'd trade the trials of not enough for the trials of too much any day."

Because we are prone to think that way, we can be susceptible to any number of tactics that promise to build our bank accounts. Our desire for the ease we believe that money will bring can wreak havoc on our powers of discernment. For that reason, Proverbs backs up the truth of this saying: "If it sounds too good to be true, it is." Get-rich-quick schemes don't work, and those who repeatedly latch onto them are those who allow greed to drown out the voice of wisdom. This includes those who use much-needed income to purchase lottery tickets or to invest in high-risk stocks or business ventures rather than paying the mortgage or the electric bill.

> The plans of the diligent lead surely to abundance,
> but everyone who is hasty comes only to poverty.
> (Prov. 21:5)

> Wealth gained hastily will dwindle,
> but whoever gathers little by little will increase it.
> (Prov. 13:11)

When the housing market collapsed in 2008, people couldn't pass the blame around fast enough. In keeping with the mind-set of our society, the media centered most of its outrage on Wall Street, the government, and mortgage lenders but had very little to say about individual culpability. While it is true that all those institutions contributed to the housing downfall, equally to blame were the thousands upon thousands who took out mortgages they couldn't afford. It was unbiblical when the government claimed that every American has a "right" to own a home, and it was unbiblical when mortgage lenders told people that their dream house could be had for no money down. But equally unbiblical were those who wanted it so badly that they signed on the dotted line and pushed away any thought that they might be undertaking something way beyond their financial means. Some careful investigation and the obtaining of wise advice would have prevented countless foreclosures. It was greed that got in the way and won out over wisdom across the American board.

our heart's treasure

That being said, Proverbs' primary emphasis when it comes to finances is less about our intellectual grasp of fiscal issues than about the place it holds in our heart. The heart is, in large part, what makes the difference between riches and poverty in one's life. God's providence, of course, is the overarching factor, but it is his very providence that has determined that our hearts play a part in our financial well-being. Nevertheless, God's will isn't that we go to Proverbs as we would to a personal financial advisor. No, in all our wealth or poverty, whether arrived at through wisdom or folly, his objective is to wean us from caring overly much about money altogether and to teach us to depend on him for all our needs, including the provision of wisdom. Agur, who wrote the sayings found in chapter 30 of Proverbs, prayed:

> Remove far from me falsehood and lying;
>> give me neither poverty nor riches;
>> feed me with the food that is needful for me,
> lest I be full and deny you
>> and say, "Who is the LORD?"
> or lest I be poor and steal
>> and profane the name of my God. (Prov. 30:8–9)

What are we to make, then, of this proverb?

> A rich man's wealth is his strong city;
>> the poverty of the poor is their ruin. (Prov. 10:15)

From these particular proverbs, we can learn something important about the book of Proverbs. Its sayings aren't so much promises as they are observations about how life works. If we can grasp this, we can learn how to apply its teachings correctly. Proverbs 10:15 is a good example. The writer is making an observation that those with money tend to have it easier in some ways than those who don't. None of us would disagree with that, which is why we are so tempted to set our hearts on acquiring it. When a home repair becomes necessary, money in the bank keeps us from the worry of how to pay for it. When our son wants to attend that pricey summer camp, a healthy bank account enables us to experience the joy of saying yes. When a friend asks us to join her in Hawaii for a week, our money enables us to feel anticipation unalloyed by guilt when we click "purchase" on the Orbitz website. Money can indeed be a blessing, which is exactly what Proverbs 10:15 is acknowledging.

Nevertheless, throughout the Bible we are warned against the lure of seeking our security in money. Paul wrote, "The love of money is a root of all kinds of evils" (1 Tim. 6:10). The danger is found in the very blessing that money provides—a sense of security. And the reason it's dangerous is, first, that God alone deserves our trust; and, second, we ultimately have no control over our personal security. That's why Proverbs also says:

> Do not toil to acquire wealth;
>   be discerning enough to desist.
> When your eyes light on it, it is gone,
>   for suddenly it sprouts wings,
>   flying like an eagle toward heaven. (Prov. 23:4–5)

This is actually good news, because most of us will never be wealthy anyway. It is good news because we have been offered something so much better to rely on—God himself. Jesus said, "Therefore I tell you, do not be anxious about your life, what you will eat or what you will drink, nor about your body, what you will put on. Is not life more than food, and the body more than clothing? Look at the birds of the air: they neither sow nor reap nor gather into barns, and yet your heavenly Father feeds them. Are you not of more value than they?" (Matt. 6:25–26). And the writer of Hebrews wrote, "Keep your life free from love of money, and be content with what you have, for [God] has said, 'I will never leave you nor forsake you'" (Heb. 13:5).

It is also good news because many of us have made a mess of managing our money, and we are living with the consequences of it even now. But God doesn't shape our lives around our financial savvy or successes or failures. He shapes them around his own plans, and those plans include even the messes we make. J. I. Packer writes:

> The reason why the Bible spends so much of its time reiterating that God is a strong rock, a firm defense, and a sure refuge and help for the weak, is that God spends so much of His time bringing home to us that we are weak, both mentally and morally, and dare not trust ourselves to find, or to follow, the right road. . . . And God wants us to feel that our way through life is rough and per-plexing, so that we may learn thankfully to lean on Him. . . . God actually uses our sins and mistakes to this end. He employs the educative discipline of failures and mistakes very frequently. . . . God can bring good out of the extremes of our own folly; God can restore the years that the locust has eaten. . . . Is your trouble a sense of failure? the knowledge of having made some ghastly mistake? Go back to God; His restoring grace waits for you.[1]

In God's economy, there are far more important things to pursue than money, such as righteousness and the blessings of acquiring a reputation that brings glory to him:

> Whoever trusts in his riches will fall,
> but the righteous will flourish like a green leaf.
> (Prov. 11:28)

> A good name is to be chosen rather than great riches,
> and favor is better than silver or gold. (Prov. 22:1)

Because God's agenda for us is different from the world's, we are wise to keep upper-income-bracket potential from being the primary determiner in our choice of career or spouse. And also we can let go of our regrets over past financial mistakes and get on with what really matters. Are you living with monetary regret of one sort or another? If so, take it to God and ask him to transform you through it and bring good out of it. He will do so. Whatever our financial past or present may be, its future can be governed by wisdom, and a good first step is making the prayer of Agur our own. Will you?

the world . . .

"I doubt that fidelity is absolutely essential for a relationship. Neither Brad nor I have ever claimed that living together means being chained together."

—Angelina Jolie, *Das Neue* magazine

the word . . .

Drink water from your own cistern,
flowing water from your own well.
Should your springs be scattered abroad,
streams of water in the streets?
Let them be for yourself alone,
and not for strangers with you.
Let your fountain be blessed,
and rejoice in the wife of your youth.

—Proverbs 5:15–18

CHAPTER 8

wise women safeguard their sexuality

In a society where gay marriage and the practice of pedophilia are being argued as rights, it's hard to believe that adultery is still illegal in some states. We find this on the law books in Minnesota:

> When a married woman has sexual intercourse with a man other than her husband, whether married or not, both are guilty of adultery and may be sentenced to imprisonment for not more than one year or to payment of a fine of not more than $3,000, or both.[1]

The reason we are unaware of such laws is that they aren't enforced; they are used primarily as negotiating tools in divorce settlements.[2] But what matters to us is not so much what the law books say about sexual practices as what God's Word says.

Sex is a major theme in the book of Proverbs. The original intention of this sex education was to instruct young men about what sort of woman to seek and what sort to avoid. Even though the original audience was male, we women can learn a lot from it too. First, as we consider Proverbs' teaching about the difference between the nice girls and those who aren't so nice, we can examine our hearts to make sure we are the right sort. Second, because we live in a society where women have freedom like no other women in history, the advice in Proverbs about what to guard against isn't applicable only to men today.

Back when Proverbs was compiled, women weren't independent as they are now. They pretty much went from the home of their parents to the home of their husband without experiencing the interim seasons of dorm or apartment life as do young women today. Additionally, the initial consequences for sexual sin in ancient Israel were far more dire than they are today, which served as a deterrent. So, although we enjoy greater independence now, with that freedom comes more opportunity for temptation and sexual sin.

As we delve into all that Proverbs has to say on the subject, we want to ask ourselves how we can be the sort of woman that the young male readers of the proverbs were being advised to seek. We also want to become wise about how to deal with our own temptations when it comes to sex and to understand where and when they arise and how to master them.

why is sex outside of marriage so bad anyway?

Sexual sin, like all other sin, springs from the heart, and it can explode into actions and infect our thoughts, our words, and our deeds. The fool allows the hidden immorality in her heart to break out into open sexual sins. But is sexual sin really so bad? That question hits everyone at some point, and not just unbelievers. After all, unbelievers aren't the only ones having affairs and questioning the legitimacy of heterosexual-only marriage. There are professing Christians living in unrepentant sexual sin who have also asked that question and answered it in the negative.

But it is bad. Really bad. For one thing, it's a violation of God's creation order. God didn't design marriage only for Christians; he established it at the time of creation for all people. Marriage—the joining of one man to one woman in a lifelong commitment—was set up by God for mankind in general. As for believers specifically, there is something about sexual sin in particular that violates our union with Christ, as we see from something Paul wrote to the Corinthians:

> The body is not meant for sexual immorality, but for the Lord, and the Lord for the body. And God raised the Lord and will also raise us up by his power. Do you not know that your bodies are members of Christ? Shall I then take the members of Christ and make them members of a prostitute? Never! Or do you not know that he who is joined to a prostitute becomes one body with her? For, as it is written, "The two will become one flesh." But he who is joined to the Lord becomes one spirit with him. (1 Cor. 6:13–17)

In some mystical way, we become one with whomever we have sexual intercourse. And Paul seems to be saying that this becoming one is more than just a physical oneness; there is a spiritual component too.

The consequences of sexual sin bear this out. Consider the fact that sexual sin is destructive in one way or another, physically, relationally, and always spiritually. As we noted earlier, Paul makes clear in Romans 1 that sexual sin issues from hearts that reject God, and those who do not forsake it grow increasingly perverse in their sexual desires. It leads to spiritual insanity.

Sexual sin is bad also because it blocks the process of our sanctification:

> This is the will of God, your sanctification: that you abstain from sexual immorality; that each one of you know how to control his own body in holiness and honor, not in the passion of lust like the Gentiles who do not know God; that no one transgress and wrong his brother in this matter, because the Lord is an avenger in all these things, as we told you beforehand and solemnly warned you. For God has not called us for impurity, but in holiness. Therefore whoever disregards this, disregards not man but God, who gives his Holy Spirit to you. (1 Thess. 4:3–8)

Nowhere in Scripture do we read that sex is okay if you love someone enough. Nor do we find passages that address the oft asked question, "How far can I go before it's sinful?" To even ask this question is to reveal a divided heart, because undivided hearts aren't thinking along those lines at all. An undivided heart asks instead, "How holy can I be?"

Proverbs 5 and 7 warn susceptible young men not to get seduced by a certain type of woman. She is dangerous, although her danger is hidden beneath charming lies:

> For the lips of a forbidden woman drip honey,
> and her speech is smoother than oil. (Prov. 5:3)

In other words, she knows how to turn a man on, and she has no scruples about going after the men she wants. People—all of us—can be flattered when someone finds us attractive, and the Devil knows that this sort of appeal to our ego is enormous. Temptation to sexual sin is most often going to hit us, whether we are male or female, smack in the ego, and there are terrible consequences for giving in:

- Loss of honor (Prov. 5:9)
- Life's labors taken away and used by others (Prov. 5:10)
- Loss of strength and character (Prov. 7:22–23, 26)
- Ongoing physical consequences (Prov. 5:11)
- Regret (Prov. 5:12–14)
- Death (Prov. 7:26–27)
- Divine judgment (Prov. 5:21)

Yes, sexual sin is really that bad.

the immoral woman

Character references to the immoral woman, also called the "forbidden woman" and the "adulteress," are sprinkled throughout Proverbs, and there are two large sections in the book that paint a fuller picture:

The lips of a forbidden woman drip honey,
    and her speech is smoother than oil,
but in the end she is bitter as wormwood,
    sharp as a two-edged sword.
Her feet go down to death;
    her steps follow the path to Sheol;
she does not ponder the path of life;
    her ways wander, and she does not know it.
And now, O sons, listen to me,
    and do not depart from the words of my mouth.
Keep your way far from her,
    and do not go near the door of her house,
lest you give your honor to others
    and your years to the merciless,
lest strangers take their fill of your strength,
    and your labors go to the house of a foreigner,
and at the end of your life you groan,
    when your flesh and body are consumed,
and you say, "How I hated discipline,
    and my heart despised reproof!
I did not listen to the voice of my teachers
    or incline my ear to my instructors.
I am at the brink of utter ruin
    in the assembled congregation." (Prov. 5:3–14)

At the window of my house
    I have looked out through my lattice,
and I have seen among the simple,
    I have perceived among the youths,
    a young man lacking sense,
passing along the street near her corner,
    taking the road to her house
in the twilight, in the evening,
    at the time of night and darkness.
And behold, the woman meets him,
    dressed as a prostitute, wily of heart.
She is loud and wayward;
    her feet do not stay at home;

> now in the street, now in the market,
>> and at every corner she lies in wait.
> She seizes him and kisses him,
>> and with bold face she says to him,
> "I had to offer sacrifices,
>> and today I have paid my vows;
> so now I have come out to meet you,
>> to seek you eagerly, and I have found you.
> I have spread my couch with coverings,
>> colored linens from Egyptian linen;
> I have perfumed my bed with myrrh,
>> aloes, and cinnamon.
> Come, let us take our fill of love till morning;
>> let us delight ourselves with love.
> For my husband is not at home;
>> he has gone on a long journey;
> he took a bag of money with him;
>> at full moon he will come home."
> With much seductive speech she persuades him;
>> with her smooth talk she compels him. (Prov. 7:6–21)

Taking a close look at the immoral woman in Proverbs teaches us a lot about our own hearts. We are likely to discover that we have more of her in us than we'd like to believe.

First, we discover that she is a *discontented* woman:

> She is loud and wayward;
>> her feet do not stay at home. (Prov. 7:11)

A discontented woman is always looking for something different from what she already has. She wants something that she believes God hasn't provided. We see her in the single woman who is desperate for a husband and in the married women who wants a different husband or a more perfect marriage. Whatever our situation, we can be sure that discontentment has set in whenever we find ourselves thinking, "God didn't do right by me, so I'll get what I want anyway." Oh, we don't think or say it quite like that. But however we spin it, we are doing it whenever we seek satisfaction in our own way by our own means.

The second thing we notice about her is that she *fuels her lust*:

> Come, let us take our fill of love till morning;
> let us delight ourselves with love. (Prov. 7:18)

Lust is typically thought of as a man's issue, but that's incorrect. Lust is not a gender issue; it's an *opportunity* issue. Men or women exposed to or exposing themselves to sexual stimuli are going to lust. If the protections are lifted, or if we lift them, we will lust. And if we feed lustful thoughts and desires, before long they will break out into acts of open immorality.

Third, Proverbs reveals that the immoral woman *seeks to get what and whom she wants with her speech*. Young men are advised to embrace wisdom so that they won't fall victim to "the adulteress with her smooth words" (2:16ff.). Such a woman has no compunction about trying to attract and draw the attention of other women's husbands. Perhaps you've felt the sting of jealousy because another woman has, in one way or another, drawn the attention of your husband. It's an awful feeling! But are we never guilty of doing the same thing ourselves? We might be at times, without recognizing that we are doing it.

This can be a special danger in an office setting, where men and women work side by side and spend more of their waking hours with their colleagues than with their spouses. For the working women among us, are we careful what we do with such close proximity? It is to be hoped that we conscientiously avoid flirtatious repartee with our married coworkers, but do we do all we can to safeguard our married colleagues from temptation? Office banter can be a slippery slope, as can having discussions about our personal lives—or about theirs. Working together is a bonding experience, and, naturally, friendships arise. But because this is so, it is all the more reason to guard our words in the office.

The "smooth words" of Proverbs 2:16 are perhaps best understood as flattering words. As we examined earlier, this is the sort of talk that all people, both men and women, are susceptible to, because flatterers aim their words directly at the perceived weaknesses of others. Flatterers are always after something from those they flatter, and if we are not finding our satisfaction in God's provision and in God himself, the words of a flatterer can be our downfall into sexual sin. How about you? Are you susceptible to the flattery of a man to whom you are not married? We are likely to be susceptible to the flattery of unavailable men if their words stroke us in an area of personal disappointment or failure, or in an area where we have felt let down by our husbands.

The immoral woman is also characterized by *a refusal to think seriously about life*:

> She does not ponder the path of life;
> her ways wander, and she does not know it. (Prov. 5:6)

The proverb isn't saying that those with a happy-go-lucky personality are prone to immorality. It is making a link between immorality and a woman who avoids using her mind altogether. "The general sense is that her ways are *shifty* and *slippery* . . . in order to keep serious thought at bay," writes Derek Kidner.[3] Lots of things are hard to think about—painful losses and difficult decisions we must make and ongoing difficulties that just never seem to change—and the grind of daily life can be overwhelming sometimes. But wise women, those who live in humble trust in God, are able to face their realities with contentment and discover more facets of God's good character along the way. Those who refuse to grapple with life's hard things are rejecting God, and in the process they turn to a god of their own making as a way of escape from the difficulties.

Sexual pleasure is a common escape—just ask anyone who's cheated on her spouse during a difficult time in her marriage. Or just ask the twenty-something single who, abandoned by her father during childhood, has already slept with more men than she can count. Or ask the porn addict whose addiction began by surfing the web as an escape from loneliness. They are not pondering the path of life, and their ways are wandering.

We also see that the immoral activities of the woman in Proverbs are *done in the dark*:

> At the window of my house
>   I have looked out through my lattice,
> and I have seen among the simple,
>   I have perceived among the youths,
>   a young man lacking sense,
> passing along the street near her corner,
>   taking the road to her house
> in the twilight, in the evening,
>   at the time of night and darkness. (Prov. 7:6–9)

Immoral behavior is done in the dark; in other words, there is always a secretive nature to it. Here is an area where self-examination shouldn't prove too difficult. Any encounter or activity that we feel we must hide or about which we must prevaricate even just a bit is likely not a good one. If something is honorable and right, light can shine on it with full force with nary a qualm in our hearts. Any reticence to reveal is a tip-off that something is wrong.

how not to be like her

So how do we avoid becoming like her? Or, if we have realized that we already resemble her, how can we change?

First, we can learn to recognize what draws our hearts toward temptation. For some of us, it's the desire to be wanted or to be seen as attractive—the lust to be lusted after. Our temptation may be not so much sex itself but wanting to be considered as a turn-on to others. For others among us, however, it's just plain old lust, and the avoidance tactic here is simple: don't do it. Don't think about it. Don't fantasize.

Temptation might come to others through a strong desire to escape an uncomfortable daily reality, and toying with something morally shady seems like a reasonable way to cope with the tension until the situation gets better. What can trip us up here is the temptation—the lie—that escaping by means of an illicit flirtation or conversation or dalliance is safe because no one will know. That's exactly what the immoral woman in Proverbs 7 told herself.

> Come, let us take our fill of love till morning;
>> let us delight ourselves with love.
> For my husband is not at home;
>> he has gone on a long journey. (Prov. 7:18–19)

We must be on guard for whatever appeals to us as a means of getting a need met quickly, quietly, in a small corner of our lives that we kid ourselves into believing won't disrupt any other corner. It will always without exception disrupt a lot more than a corner or two.

We can also avoid becoming like the immoral woman of Proverbs by recognizing the power of sexual sin. There is valuable wisdom in such knowledge, which need not (and hopefully will not) come about from personal experience. All it takes is the willingness to accept the reality of how very sinful sin is and that in this life we will never get past it.

> Many a victim has she laid low,
>> and all her slain are a mighty throng. (Prov. 7:26)

Those of us who have not known firsthand the destruction of sexual sin nevertheless have surely witnessed it, if not among our family or friends, then certainly in the media. It breaks apart hearts and families; it ruins careers; it destroys lives. In light of the very tangible consequences, the fact that so many still fall prey is testimony to its power. The sex drive is probably the strongest drive that human beings experience.

But the pull toward sexual expression isn't the only reason that people are drawn in. "Many a victim has she laid low," says Proverbs. Another translation has "She has cast down many wounded" (NKJV). People who fall morally are victims of their basic sin nature and natural urges, but some are also victims of the sin of others. Many promiscuous young women have suffered parental abandonment or abuse, as have the majority of women in the porn industry. The "victim" of verse 26 is someone harmed by sin, whether her own or that of another.

The primary way we avoid becoming like the immoral woman is by *fleeing temptation* and the things that fan it into flame. That's what Joseph had to do when he was solicited by Potiphar's wife, who "cast her eyes on Joseph and said, 'Lie with me'" (Gen. 39:7). Joseph was in a position where actually running away could have cost him his life (as is unlikely to be the case with us), but eventually he felt he had no other choice because the woman was persistent in her pursuit (v. 10), and run away he did. The Bible doesn't tell us why Joseph ran, but it might have been because this wanton woman was wearing down his resolve. Whether tempted or not, he fled the situation at risk of his life, and indeed he did suffer as a result of his obedience to God. We can be sure however that he had no long-term regrets.

Paul put it in no uncertain terms: "Flee from sexual immorality" (1 Cor. 6:18). So how exactly do we flee our own particular temptations to sexual sin? One way we flee is by being careful not to give an impression to others that we are open to the possibility. Sexual signals aren't difficult to pick up on. There is a sort of sexual radar that seems to be hardwired into people, both men and women.

Another way to flee is by steering clear of provocative forms of entertainment. If we lack a fast-forward option, perhaps we can skip certain movies altogether. I mean, really. What good can come of watching that heavy make-out session or graphic sex scene?

It is also wise to be selective in the company we keep. Have we been getting an illicit read on our sexual radar in the company of a certain someone? If so, and especially if we realize we have kicked into radar-response mode, our course of action is clear—get out of there. Leave the room or the relationship itself, if necessary. If we catch it as this stage, there is no way it can advance.

Sometimes as we contemplate fleeing, the negative ramifications of doing so rise up in our minds, so rather than making a radical move, we simply determine to tune out the temptation. Occasionally that works; often it does not. We cannot go wrong following Paul's guidance, no matter the outcome. Remember Joseph.

> Keep your way far from her,
>> and do not go near the door of her house. (Prov. 5:8)

Being wise in this sort of situation involves more than just knowing what the Bible says about it. After all, Christians who fall in this area usually *do* know what the Bible says, but they have given into temptation anyway. The wisdom we need to avoid falling into sexual sin is the fear of the Lord. The best way to flee temptation is to cultivate an abiding trust in God that is rooted in the conviction that the path of holiness he has marked out for each one of us will lead to mental, emotional, and spiritual prosperity. That is the fear of the Lord in action.

safeguarding marriage

Wise women, whether married or single, recognize that sexual sin is a violation of marriage, and for that reason they seek to safeguard not only their own marriage but also that of others.

The first safeguard is to *acknowledge that safeguards are*

necessary, because no one is above a fall into sexual sin. Both men and women are susceptible, and that includes Christian men and women. It is the height of folly to think that just because we are believers or have a successful ministry we are above it. In fact, those most likely to fall are those who are convinced that they'll never fall. "Let anyone who thinks that he stands take heed lest he fall," Paul wrote (1 Cor. 10:12). How many times have we heard people say, upon hearing of a believer having an affair, "How could that have happened? I thought she was a Christian!" The truth is, we do think Christians are less tempted to sin in this way, but if that were true, the Bible, which is written specifically to God's people, wouldn't be filled with so many warnings about it.

Adultery is a direct attack on marriage, not merely a violation of it; it is the willful ripping apart of a God-ordained union. And the outcome of adultery is always bitter. Have you ever heard of an adulterous relationship that didn't result in bitterness? What we see in the world around us and in our own experiences bears out the truth of that. So does God's Word:

> He who commits adultery lacks sense;
>> he who does it destroys himself.
> He will get wounds and dishonor,
>> and his disgrace will not be wiped away. (Prov. 6:32–33)

There is nothing as damaging to a marriage as adultery. Jesus said, "Everyone who divorces his wife, except on the ground of sexual immorality, makes her commit adultery, and whoever marries a divorced woman commits adultery" (Matt. 5:32). His words imply that sexual sin can utterly destroy a marriage. And if divorce does occur as a result, God is grieved. Jesus may have given an out to a betrayed spouse, but that doesn't mean that taking the out is pleasing to God. He is never pleased by divorce, no matter the cause, which places the betrayed spouse in a terrible dilemma: either to remain in a broken marriage with no trust or to leave the marriage and grieve God. Regardless of whether the marriage stays intact, the outcome of adultery is bitter.

The parents of King Solomon, the primary author of Proverbs, were brought together as the result of an adulterous relationship. Solomon's mother, Bathsheba, was married to a man named Uriah, but she slept with King David, Solomon's father, while Uriah was away serving in the military. Bathsheba got pregnant as a result, and David hatched a plot to keep Uriah from finding out. But the plot failed, so David had Uriah killed in battle. It was all for nothing anyway. God judged the adulterous act by allowing Bathsheba's baby to die. You can read all about it in 2 Samuel 11. Adultery leads always to lies and loss—100 percent of the time. Since none of us is above it, therefore, the first safeguard we erect is the humble admission that we aren't above it.

The second safeguard is to *cultivate gratitude for our marriage* and for marriage in general.

> Let your fountain be blessed,
>> and rejoice in the wife of your youth,
>> a lovely deer, a graceful doe.
> Let her breasts fill you at all times with delight;
>> be intoxicated always in her love. (Prov. 5:18–20)

"Easier said than done," you might be thinking. "You don't have *my* husband." But that's not the point. Very likely, many of the men seeking to follow the instruction in the proverb weren't married to a lovely deer or a graceful doe either. The teacher wasn't trying to be an idealistic Pollyanna. Most likely he was guiding his pupils about the importance of viewing their spouse in a specific light, and we can do the same. Your husband might not be the Prince Charming you thought early on, but you chose to marry him for a reason. What was it? Think back. Call to mind his good qualities and focus on them rather than clinging to the disappointments and qualities that you find so irritating now.

Do you struggle with this? Most married people do at one point or another, but God, who loves to bless what he has ordained, will help you renew your marital delight if you are willing to be helped.

Whenever I am struggling with discontentment, I've found that the way out of it begins with practicing gratitude. Lately my struggle has involved my living quarters. I live in a multi-family dwelling, and my upstairs neighbor is heavy footed. He is also young, which means he has the energy to stay out until 2 a.m. both weekend nights and once or twice during the week. I, on the other hand, am a light sleeper who, not being young, thinks being awake at 10 p.m. constitutes a late night. The differences in our lifestyles could so easily create neighborly discord, but by God's grace we get along fine. I express my gratitude to God for that. And I call to mind the time that this neighbor collected my mail when I forgot to have it held at the post office before a trip, and another time when he took my discarded Christmas tree down to the curb after the holiday. And I recall that he did two tours in Iraq as a Marine. I also pray for him, and I've found that if I pray when I am most annoyed, the annoyance dissipates. Praying for someone is an act of love, and irritation tends to melt away before love in action.

If all this sounds just a little bit pious, let me be quick to add that recalling positive qualities and even praying for another in the midst of relational difficulty overcomes discontentment only because it is done in the fear of the Lord. In other words, it is an outworking of clinging to Christ in the midst of the difficulty and becoming transformed in the process. Through our union with Christ, we will find we are increasingly enabled to delight in those who irritate us, whether neighbor or friend or spouse, and when it comes to the spouse, there is the added dimension of God's seal over the relationship. The one who ordained marriage in general ordained yours in particular, and he cares more about your marital health than about any other human relationship you have. He is not blind to the difficulties, big and small. He is not oblivious to your loss of respect for your husband or the hurt you feel because your husband has stopped communicating with you. Whatever the issue may be, you will be enabled to live in peace and value your marriage—even when you see no change—if you cling to Christ rather than clinging to your ideals for your spouse and your marriage. If your marriage is hard, value it anyway, because God values it.

Married or single, we all are called to value marriage simply because God values it. This can be difficult not only for women in a struggling marriage but also for single women who long to be married. The very idea that they are supposed to value and protect something they cannot have can breed resentment. Nevertheless, wise women, married or single, value marriage.

Another important safeguard for marriage—our own and that of others—is *immersing ourselves in God's Word*:

> For the commandment is a lamp and the teaching a light,
>   and the reproofs of discipline are the way of life,
> to preserve you from the evil woman,
>   from the smooth tongue of the adulteress.
>   (Prov. 6:23–24)

It takes humility to recognize and admit that we can fall in these ways apart from dependence on the Holy Spirit and Scripture. We're not strong enough to withstand certain temptations on our own, and neither is the best of marriages.

The fourth safeguard is *don't buy into the lie that no one will get hurt*.

> Can a man carry fire next to his chest
>   and his clothes not be burned?
> Or can one walk on hot coals
>   and his feet not be scorched?

> So is he who goes in to his neighbor's wife;
>> none who touches her will go unpunished.
>> (Prov. 6:27–29)

When adultery occurs, someone always gets hurt. In the short run it is usually just the betrayed spouse and the children of the broken marriage. In the long run it is also the cheating spouse and his or her partner, for not only was their relationship forged on illicit grounds, but also is comprised of two people with blatantly immoral character. The bottom line is this: if a woman abandons her husband because she doesn't feel in love anymore, that is immoral. If she claims that her actions have God's approval because God just wants her to be happy, that is blasphemous.

The fifth safeguard is to cultivate within your marriage *a healthy and active sex life*.

> Drink water from your own cistern,
>> flowing water from your own well.
> Should your springs be scattered abroad,
>> streams of water in the streets?
> Let them be for yourself alone,
>> and not for strangers with you.
> Let your fountain be blessed,
>> and rejoice in the wife of your youth,
>> a lovely deer, a graceful doe.
> Let her breasts fill you at all times with delight;
>> be intoxicated always in her love. (Prov. 5:15–19)

Scripture is not prudish. In fact, in places it is quite graphic about sex, such as in the Song of Solomon. And the apostle Paul candidly instructed husbands and wives not to withhold themselves from one another: "The husband should give to his wife her conjugal rights, and likewise the wife to her husband" (1 Cor. 7:3). And he gives the reason why: "Because of the temptation to sexual immorality, each man should have his own wife and each woman her own husband"

(v. 2). Proverbs 5:15–19 is providing the same instruction, which is made clear from the very next verse: "Why should you be intoxicated, my son, with a forbidden woman and embrace the bosom of an adulteress?" (v. 20). Derek Kidner writes, "It is highly important to see sexual delight in marriage as God-given; and history confirms that when marriage is viewed chiefly as a business arrangement, not only is God's bounty misunderstood, but human passion seeks (cf. verse 20) other outlets."[4] The way to avoid temptations to sexual sin is to enjoy sex with your own spouse.

This sort of instruction can be discouraging to those who, for one reason or another, are experiencing a season in which sex is something to be endured rather than delighted in. This is not uncommon for women coping with the exhaustion of caring for an infant or for women going through menopause, and all couples go through seasons where sex is just the same old routine. But that's life—not just in your marriage but in all of them. Perhaps God didn't intend for that hot, panting, burning passion that characterized the first year of your marriage to last forever. If it did, you might never have gotten out of bed to take on the responsibilities of daily life. Because we humans are so naturally self-centered, perhaps God designed that initial passion simply to get us into marriage. Apart from that sexual tension, there are many who might never be willing to walk down the aisle and embrace the death to self-interest that marriage necessitates.

So, if that's the case, isn't this particular marital safeguard a bit idealistic? It is not, since it is God's Word that deems it a safeguard. Perhaps we just need to view it a bit differently. We might be picturing the "delight" of Proverbs 5:19 as feelings of intense sexual passion, but why fixate there? Is there not delight simply in the oneness and intimacy and in the fact that, by God's design, sex promotes love? If what was required for delightful marriage is two people who can't keep their hands off each other, then neither Proverbs nor Paul would have felt compelled to instruct spouses to continue to come together in a sexual way. We will find delight if we drink water from our own cistern, with or without panting passion.

Sometimes, of course, there are impediments, and some women have no cisterns at all. But none of us is really left with no well, because Jesus is our ultimate and permanent well. To the woman who had gone through five husbands plus a live-in and had never found what she was seeking, he said, "If you knew the gift of God . . . you would have asked him, and he would have given you living water" (John 4:10). He is our living water, and there we can drink deeply, no matter our marital status. We can rest in him where our marriage falls short. We can rest in him if we *have* no marriage. When we drink from this well, we will find all we need to resist looking for love in all the wrong places.

The sixth safeguard is to *cultivate godly jealousy*. In other words, be protective of your marriage. Don't allow others into the intimate space you share with your spouse. We think of jealousy as sinful, and it is when it springs from a craving to get something that belongs to someone else. It is not sinful when it's about protecting what God has given to us. Godly jealousy functions like an indicator light on the dashboard that begins to glow red when something is amiss in the engine. Jealousy for our marriage mirrors God's jealousy for his people. Throughout the Old Testament we see that God is furiously jealous when his people cheat on him with other gods (see, e.g., Deut. 32:16; 1 Kings 14:22; Ps. 78:58; Ezek. 5:13), and his anger at being betrayed is reflected in the anger of the betrayed husband in Proverbs:

> For jealousy makes a man furious,
> and he will not spare when he takes revenge. (Prov. 6:34)

A young pastor and his wife invited a struggling young woman to live in their home for an indefinite period of time. But she was an attractive young woman, and while the intentions all the way around were good, the whole set-up was a bad idea. A month into the arrangement, the wife expressed to me her discomfort with it. I suggested she go home and share her discomfort with her husband immediately, which she did, and together they helped the young woman relocate before that week was over. The wife's jealousy was good and right, and so was the husband's response. Together they learned a wise and practical lesson: barring any other reasonable option (not ideal necessarily, but reasonable), a young, attractive woman ought not come to live with a married couple.

Another couple I know about is going through a dark time in their marriage. A few months back the wife confessed to her husband her struggle with homosexual feelings, and ever since her confession they have been trying to navigate their way through her troubling admission. Recently, however, she has developed a close friendship with a woman who shares her struggle. The husband is rightly jealous but afraid to say so because his wife's new friendship has lifted her moodiness. He would be wise to express that jealousy posthaste and without reserve.

Immorality, whether before, during, or after marriage, whether mental, emotional, or physical, is always rebellion against God. Christians can and do fall. And in reality, we are all guilty to varying degrees. Do you think you are not? Just look at Jesus's words in Matthew: "You have heard that it was said, 'You shall not commit adultery.' But I say to you that everyone who looks at a woman with lustful intent has already committed adultery with her in his heart" (Matt. 5:27–28). Have you never looked at someone with lustful thoughts? Perhaps you are the rare exception who never has. But look at what the Westminster Larger Catechism has to say about it and see if you aren't more like the immoral woman of Proverbs than perhaps you had realized:

> The duties required in the seventh commandment are chastity in body, mind, affections, words, and behavior; and the

preservation of it in ourselves and others; watchfulness over the eyes and all the senses; temperance, keeping of chaste company, modesty in apparel; marriage by those who have not the gift of continency, conjugal love, and cohabitation [living together in marriage]; diligent labor in our callings; shunning all occasions of uncleanliness, and resisting temptations thereunto. The sins forbidden in the seventh commandment, besides neglect of the duties required, are adultery, fornication, rape, incest, sodomy, and all unnatural lusts; all unclean imaginations, thoughts, purposes, and affections; all corrupt or filthy communications, or listening thereunto; wanton looks, impudent or light behavior, immodest apparel; prohibiting of lawful and dispensing with unlawful marriages; entangling vows of single life, undue delay of marriage . . . unjust divorce or desertion; idleness, gluttony, drunkenness, unchaste company; lascivious songs, books, pictures, dancing, stage plays, and all other provocations to or acts of uncleanness, either in ourselves or others.

In light of this, what are we to do? We all are or have been the immoral woman in one way or another. If anything in that description fits our present state, we do well to consider what Jesus told the adulterous woman who was dragged before him: "Has no one condemned you? . . . Neither do I condemn you; go, and from now on sin no more" (John 8:10–11).

Perhaps there is something in the catechism that describes an earlier time in our personal history, a particular sin of which we repented long ago. If so, we can consider the women whom God placed in the lineage of Jesus. There was Tamar, who pretended to be a prostitute and slept with her father-in-law. There was Rahab, who actually was a prostitute. And there was Bathsheba, who had a liaison with the king while her husband was away. All three had a sordid past, but later they were given an honored place in redemptive history.

If you are filled with regret over past sexual sin and believe that you must forfeit future blessings and usefulness in God's service, just look at something that God promised to his people if they would repent of their spiritual adultery:

> I will restore to you the years
>   that the swarming locust has eaten,
> the hopper, the destroyer, and the cutter,
>   my great army, which I sent among you.
> You shall eat in plenty and be satisfied,
>   and praise the name of the LORD your God,
>   who has dealt wondrously with you.
>   And my people shall never again be put to shame.
>   (Joel 2:25–26)

Concerning that passage from the prophet Joel, James Boice writes:

> We cannot undo what is done. Sin is sin, and the effects of sin often continue for long periods. But God can restore what the locusts have eaten. Opportunities may have been lost, but God can give new and even better opportunities. Friends may have been alienated and driven away, but God can give new friends and even restore many of the former ones. God can break the power of sin and restore a personal holiness and joy that would not have been dreamed of in the rebellion. Are you one whose life has been destroyed by the locusts of sin? Has sin stripped your life of every green thing, so that it seems a spiritual desert? If so, you need to return to the One who alone can make life grow fruitful again. Only God can restore the years that have been eaten away.[5]

part three

a portrait of
wisdom

An excellent wife who can find?
　　She is far more precious than jewels.
The heart of her husband trusts in her,
　　and he will have no lack of gain.
She does him good, and not harm,
　　all the days of her life.
She seeks wool and flax,
　　and works with willing hands.
She is like the ships of the merchant;
　　she brings her food from afar.
She rises while it is yet night
　　and provides food for her household
　　and portions for her maidens.
She considers a field and buys it;
　　with the fruit of her hands she plants a vineyard.
She dresses herself with strength
　　and makes her arms strong.
She perceives that her merchandise is profitable.
　　Her lamp does not go out at night.
She puts her hands to the distaff,
　　and her hands hold the spindle.
She opens her hand to the poor
　　and reaches out her hands to the needy.
She is not afraid of snow for her household,
　　for all her household are clothed in scarlet.
She makes bed coverings for herself;
　　her clothing is fine linen and purple.
Her husband is known in the gates
　　when he sits among the elders of the land.
She makes linen garments and sells them;
　　she delivers sashes to the merchant.
Strength and dignity are her clothing,
　　and she laughs at the time to come.
She opens her mouth with wisdom,
　　and the teaching of kindness is on her tongue.
She looks well to the ways of her household
　　and does not eat the bread of idleness.
Her children rise up and call her blessed;
　　her husband also, and he praises her:
"Many women have done excellently,
　　but you surpass them all."
Charm is deceitful, and beauty is vain,
　　but a woman who fears the LORD is to be praised.
Give her of the fruit of her hands,
　　and let her works praise her in the gates.

—Proverbs 31:10–31

CHAPTER 9

the woman of proverbs 31

There is a currently popular television series called *The Good Wife*. The program focuses on a character named Alicia Florrick, which is played by Julianna Margulies. In the program she is the wife of a corrupt Chicago politician. Viewing one episode is all it takes to understand the name of the series. Alicia Florrick stands by her man as he is arrested and found guilty of corruption, although as her respect for him diminishes, so do her marriage vows. One can't help but feel sorry for her. Their fictional marriage is the antithesis of the one we see in Proverbs 31, which is shown through the life of the wife.

Who is this woman, this wife, at the end of Proverbs? I've talked to many women who don't like her. She's just too perfect, and perfect people are intimidating. Perhaps you're one of those who prefer to skip right on by this last passage of Proverbs. If so, you will be glad to know she was not a real person.

Proverbs 31:10–31 is a poem set in the form of an acrostic, which means that each stanza begins with a different letter of the alphabet, in this case the Hebrew alphabet. (Psalm 119, a poem about God's Word, is set up the same way.) Poetically speaking, she is the ideal woman, and the whole point of the poem is to show young men what they should look for in a wife. Doug O'Donnell presents the poem in what is called a "chiastic" structure:

> A. The high value of an excellent wife (v. 10)
>> B. Her husband's benefits (vv. 11–12)
>>> C. Her industrious work (vv. 13–19)
>>>> D. Her doing kindness (v. 20)
>>>>> E. Fearless [of the present] (v. 21a)
>>>>>> F. Clothing her household and herself (vv. 21b–22)
>>>>>>> G. Her husband's renowned respect (v. 23)
>>>>>> F´. Clothing herself and others (vv. 24–25a)
>>>>> E´. Fearless [of the future] (v. 25b)
>>>> D´. Her teaching kindness (v. 26)
>>> C´. Her industrious work (v. 27)
>> B´. Her husband's (and children's) praise (vv. 28–29)
> A´. The high value of an excellent wife (vv. 30–31)

And then he describes the poem this way:

> Do you see how the poet takes several similar themes and, starting from both ends, works his way to the center? If we begin from the outside, the themes in the first and last lines are identical: the high value of an excellent wife. Then, as we continue to move from the outside inward, we see how the theme of an earlier section parallels a later theme. This "narrowing-in" on the main theme takes us to the center: the poetic and practical point of the passage. What is the central point of Proverbs 31:10–31? It is verse 23: "Her *husband* is known in the gates when *he* sits among the elders of the land."
>
> Now, you might think, "Her husband? How is that so? How can this poem be about 'him'? That doesn't make sense! Just look at the start and the subject of almost every sentence. Look at all those verses where 'she' is the subject—verses 12, 13, 14, 15, 16, 17, 18, 19, 20, 21, 22, 24, 25, 26, 27. This poem is not about the husband, but the wife! And then verse 23 . . . well

maybe it's just some kind of poetic digression, or maybe this 'husband' is just a foil. Yes, that's it! He's a foil to the strong, effective, and successful woman. For while 'she' is running to and fro, busy about all her work, what's 'he' doing? Sitting! He sits at the city gate. While she is working her hands to the bone—planting, buying, selling, weaving, sowing—he appears to be sitting on his."

It is natural to think this. Yet whatever our initial impression might be, we must recognize that verse 23 is no digression from the author's aim. "She" might be the main character, but "he" is the author's audience. He is the one who is to see the point of this *point*: this woman, the one described in every verse but one, is "the kind of wife a man needs in order to be successful in life." Verse 23, which declares the respect her husband receives by the most important leaders of the city—"the elders"—is no mistake. Instead, it is the bulls-eye of this poem's target, striking at the heart of its intended audience, young men. This is a book for boys; and this is a poem for boys.[1]

A man who chooses a wife like the one in the poem is wise indeed, and his life will be blessed as a result. Throughout the book of Proverbs it is more than hinted that a man's choice of a spouse can make or break him.

The same principle holds true today—a man's choice of a wife will greatly influence the course of his life. The same goes for us women. Whom we marry will largely determine where and how our lives are lived out. Overall, then, the need for wisdom when it comes to love and romance and marriage is of vital importance. Not only is this a matter of our personal well-being but also of reflecting the goodness and glory of God within our families and to those around us.

That being said, the poem isn't just for those considering marriage or those who are already married. Although she is a wife, she is most basically a woman, and a godly one at that. She is a portrait of feminine wisdom. So, as we study her, we can ask ourselves not only whether we are the type of woman a man would be wise to choose as a spouse but also, and more importantly, whether our hearts and lives reflect her wisdom no matter whether we are married, single, divorced, or widowed.

Although she is presented as the ideal woman, we won't find her intimidating if we seek to apply her to our lives in the right way. The wrong way is to take Proverbs 31:10–31 as a formula for structuring our daily lives. A simple scan of the poem's details shows it to be physically impossible, and even the opening stanza of the poem makes clear that her standards aren't easily come by:

> An excellent wife who can find?
>> She is far more precious than jewels. (Prov. 31:10)

Therefore, we do well to see the poem as an inviting challenge rather than as a condemnation of what we haven't yet achieved. What we are to glean from her is a heart attitude—what about her heart enables her to live the life she does? Her life is a picture of what happens when everything else in Proverbs is applied. She exemplifies wisdom.

A read through the poem reveals that she is part of a wealthy household. When we see that, we might be tempted to think it would be easy to be like her if only we had lots of money so that we didn't have to work as hard and could sit around and learn about wisdom, but that is to miss the point. The fact that the poem depicts her as wealthy is meant to illustrate a key point in Proverbs: those who live wisely generally prosper. In other words, wisdom is what led to wealth, not wealth to wisdom. The woman here is an illustration of what happens when life is lived out as God intended and as it's revealed throughout the entire book of Proverbs.

With that introduction in mind, let's look at the particular ways this woman portrays wisdom.

as a wife

The poem as a whole shows us she lives wisely in her marital calling, but there are only a few verses that specifically address her actual relationship with her husband. One of those verses tells us this:

> The heart of her husband trusts in her,
> and he will have no lack of gain. (Prov. 31:11)

She is trustworthy. The best way a woman can be wise in her marriage is to be someone whom others—especially her husband—can trust implicitly. Her husband can go out and do what he is called to do, knowing that the affairs of his household are safely in the hands of his wife. Her efforts will support his.

Does your husband trust you? What level of trust does he have when it comes to the family finances? Is he relaxed about your interactions with his business colleagues? Does he trust you to keep his confidences, the things he shares with you and you alone? Does he feel safe with you because you consistently build him up in his faith and in his efforts at family leadership? How about with the way you handle his failures?

Sometimes we can get so wrapped up in whether our husband is meeting our needs and with the sort of man we think he should be that we stop helping him to actually do and be all *God* has called him to be. We seek to shape our lives—and our husbands—by our expectations rather than by God's Word. A trustworthy wife is one who is concerned more about doing him good than about how much good he is doing her.

Single women do the same thing when it comes to considering prospective husbands. I've heard many a single woman complain, "All the good guys are taken!" But perhaps they haven't considered the fact that marriage done God's way is a huge component in shaping a man into one of those "good" guys. If we rule out prospective mates because they don't earn a six-figure salary, or because they don't have at least a modicum of physical resemblance to George Clooney, or because they can't conjugate a Greek verb, we do well to examine why we want a mate in the first place. Are we seeking to meet our needs, or are we seeking someone on whom to pour out love?

If we have found our path to true love frustrating, whether in marriage or before it, we'd do well to stop and consider whether our personal expectations are a contributing factor. God promises to bless, but nowhere does he promise to do so on our terms. A good first step in reorienting our spousal priorities is to toss aside our expectations. If the man in our life doesn't measure up to our laundry list of good-guy qualities, all that matters is whether he is seeking to be the sort of man Paul describes in Ephesians: "Husbands, love your wives, as Christ loved the church and gave himself up for her, that he might sanctify her, having cleansed her by the washing of water with the word, so that he might present the church to himself in splendor, without spot or wrinkle or any such thing, that she might be holy and without blemish. In the same way husbands should love their wives as their own bodies" (Eph. 5:25–28).

The qualities we find there are what matters. Single women are wise to cross off "blue eyes" and "must love cats" from their must-have list and replace those things with "demonstrates sacrificial love" and "has a desire for familial holiness." Nevertheless, wise women, whether married or single, can accept the fact that they will never have a fully formed Ephesians 5 man. The husband shown there is the ideal, just as the Proverbs 31 woman is. If a man holds out for an actual Proverbs 31 wife, chances are good he'll never marry. Just so, if we rule out any man who doesn't consistently and flawlessly live out Ephesians 5, we are going to find ourselves alone. After all, what's the point of being a helper, as God has designed us to be, if we marry someone who needs no help?

A woman who is wise in her marriage is trustworthy because she doesn't orbit around her selfish expectations. She doesn't view marriage as a self-serving vehicle for personal fulfillment, and in that way

> She does him good, and not harm,
>   all the days of her life. (Prov. 31:12)

as a household manager

Another thing that makes this woman wise is how she manages her domestic life. Several years ago I read an article in which the author said that all women are called to be homemakers. My hackles went up immediately. Where does that leave single women, I wondered? Much as we might want to, if we just quit our jobs and stay home, how will the bills get paid? I simmered over that article for days. Only later did I come to understand what the author meant—and that she was right. She wasn't pointing to homemaking as a *job* so much as she was to a *lifestyle*.

First, whether single or married, we all live somewhere. Some of us live alone; others live with family or roommates. Some of us reside in grand estates and others in studio apartments. But wherever we live, it is a home. Added to this is the fact that God designed us as nurturers, and home is a natural place to live this out, whether we expend our nurturing instinct on those within our four walls or on those who live next door. And some of us have pets to care for. I have yet to meet a woman—even among the my-career-is-my-life types—who doesn't engage in the art of domesticity.

We work out our nurturing instinct whenever we hang a picture, select a new sofa, bake a cake, or plant a garden. We do it when we put a welcome mat outside the front door, and we do it when we spend money to keep the appliances in working order. Women in particular tend more naturally to these details. Like it or not, it's the way we've been hardwired by God. Speaking personally, I like it. I find that there is something deeply gratifying about creating and maintaining a warm and comfortable home and inviting others to come share in it.

a woman's wisdom

For wives and mothers, homemaking includes not only house upkeep but also overseeing the well-being of all its occupants. That is the case with the Proverbs 31 woman, and for her it was a full-time job with plenty of overtime.

> She seeks wool and flax,
>   and works with willing hands.
> She is like the ships of the merchant;
>   she brings her food from afar. (Prov. 31:13–14)

> She rises while it is yet night
>   and provides food for her household
>   and portions for her maidens.
>   . . . Her lamp does not go out at night. (Prov. 31:15–18)

> She puts her hands to the distaff,
>   and her hands hold the spindle. (Prov. 31:19)

> She looks well to the ways of her household
>   and does not eat the bread of idleness. (Prov. 31:27)

She was busy morning, noon, and night. Here is a good place for a reminder that we are not meant to apply the poem to our lives in a literal way. Just because she got up before dawn and worked far into the night doesn't mean we must do the same in order to be godly homemakers. It's the principles that we are meant to find and apply, and one of those principles concerns the wise use of time.

She Redeems the Time

The way we *use* our time is always going to be shaped by how we *view* our time. Do we see it as a gift or as a right? Those who view time as a gift can echo the psalmist who said, "Teach us to number our days that we may get a heart of wisdom" (Ps. 90:12). They realize that their time is actually a God-given asset that they are to invest for God's glory. They are cognizant of the fact that an hour gone by can never be relived.

Conversely, those who view time as a right tend to hoard their hours for selfish pleasure and often resent having to invest energy in serving others—including God. I wept with remorse some time ago when I realized what a guilty time-hoarder I can be. I'd been living through an exceptionally busy speaking season, and on top of this a book deadline loomed. Additionally, I had growing responsibilities at my place of full-time employment. I felt utterly overwhelmed. But rather than casting myself upon Christ and resting in the strength he so willingly supplies, I began to grumble. Grumbling led me to where it always leads—straight into a brick wall. I had become paralyzed by the volume of projects on my plate and found myself unable to make headway with any of it. I came home one day and cast myself onto my bed and cried out to God, "I just can't do this anymore, Lord!" Over the next day or so he answered my cry with the conviction that my trouble had more to do with my attitude than with my workload. It wasn't his enabling that I'd really wanted. It was free time. In my desire to fill up more hours with relaxation and personal comforts, I had ceased to see that the work on my plate was a gift, as all kingdom work is. In writing and speaking, I'm not doing God any favors; he is blessing me with the privilege of getting to do it. Once I saw what had been wrought in my heart by my possessive spirit toward time, I wept that I could have been so selfish toward the Lord, who has done so much for me, and I found myself able to tackle the load afresh.

The principle here in Proverbs isn't that free time must be filled with work and that having fun is sinful. To the contrary, God takes delight in our enjoyment of life's pleasures. The principle has everything to do with our outlook: are we purposeful with our time in everything we do, whether it be work or play? Do we work hard at our work and give thought to our play? The apostle Paul wrote, "Look carefully then how you walk, not as unwise but as wise, *making the best use* of the time, because the days are evil" (Eph. 5:15–16); and, "walk in wisdom toward outsiders, making the best use of the time" (Col. 4:5). The Proverbs 31 woman makes the best use of her time, which is how she redeems it.

Redeeming our time doesn't necessarily mean checking everything off our to-do list. It might mean creating a shorter to-do list so that we can do the remaining tasks better. Redeeming our time most definitely involves giving thought to our entertainment choices. If an evening of relaxation on the couch is before us, redeeming the time means we give thought to our television viewing rather than clicking through channels with our mind in neutral. John Piper writes:

> TV still reigns as the great life-waster. The main problem with TV is not how much smut is available, though that is a problem. Just the ads are enough to sow fertile seeds of greed and lust, no matter what program you're watching. The greater problem is banality. A mind fed daily on TV diminishes. Your mind was made to know and love God. Its facility for this great calling is ruined by excessive TV. The content is so trivial and so shallow that the capacity of the mind to think worthy thoughts withers, and the capacity of the heart to feel deep emotions shrivels.[2]

We don't want to come away with the idea that leisure is really just more work in disguise. Both work and real leisure serve a God-ordained purpose in our lives. Ecclesiastes 3:1–10 tells us that every time and season has a purpose, and in that passage we find both work and leisure activities. That is something else we can point to that proves the Proverbs 31 woman wasn't a real person—her life was all work and no play! However, we learn from her that being a wise home manager involves making good use of our time.

She Nurtures
As a wise home manager, the Proverbs 31 woman is devoted to the well-being of others.

> She . . . provides food for her household
>> and portions for her maidens. (Prov. 31:15)

> She opens her hand to the poor
>> and reaches out her hands to the needy. (Prov. 31:20)

> She opens her mouth with wisdom,
>> and the teaching of kindness is on her tongue.
>>> (Prov. 31:26)

> She looks well to the ways of her household. (Prov. 31:27)

The manner in which she looks well to the ways of her household includes not only what she does but also what she says. Nurturing others is as much about our words as it is about providing a hot meal and clean clothes. The wisdom in her heart flows out on her tongue. She presents a stark contrast to this sort of wife:

> It is better to live in a corner of the housetop
>> than in a house shared with a quarrelsome wife.
>>> (Prov. 21:9; 25:24; cf. 19:13)

If there's a single verse in the poem that causes women to feel guilt, it's probably Proverbs 31:26: "She opens her mouth with wisdom, and the teaching of kindness is on her tongue." We read it, and what comes to mind is the last time we screamed like a banshee about muddy shoes on the clean floor, or when we uttered a glib "Don't make such a big deal of it" to a perplexed friend when we were in a hurry to get off the phone.

I find it interesting that the poet put it this way—"the teaching of kindness." This must mean more than simply saying kind things. It could mean that she teaches *with* kindness, but it could also mean that she teaches *about* kindness. Both are wise. We may have a long way to go, but we have the capacity to emulate her in this regard if we are in Christ, because kindness is an aspect of the fruit of Spirit (Gal. 5:23).

a woman's wisdom

As we saw in chapter 2, becoming a wise-tongued woman is all about where our hearts are. And as Jesus said, "Out of the abundance of the heart the mouth speaks" (Matt. 12:34).

The woman in Proverbs 31 exemplifies nurturing. No matter what task she is involved in, her overarching aim is the nurture of others. She provides food for those in her home, including the servants (v. 15); she extends her hand to the poor and needy (v. 20); and she watches over the ways of her household (v. 27). In our day, watching over our household includes being diligently aware of what our children are up to, not only when they go out and about but also when they're at home. Are you as technologically savvy as your teens? There are ways around the parental controls software. And do you know the identity of every one of your kids' Facebook friends (or whatever the latest social network site will be when you read this)? The technology changes at lightning speed, but keeping up with it is, today, part of what's involved in looking out for the ways of our household.

When Jesus sent out the twelve apostles, he warned, "Behold, I am sending you out as sheep in the midst of wolves, so be wise as serpents and innocent as doves" (Matt. 10:16). His words weren't just applicable to the apostles; they are meant for all believers. The Serpent in the garden of Eden was pretty slick, even though in an evil way. Nevertheless, he was shrewd about people and his surroundings. The takeaway here is that wise women are to be innocent of sin but not naive—and perhaps nowhere more so than when it comes to our kids.

A friend of mine, Ruby, recently found a pack of cigarettes in the handbag of her teen daughter Justine. When confronted, Justine denied ownership of the cigarettes and claimed that she was just holding them for a friend. Because of Ruby's great love for Justine, Paul's words about love come easily so far as her daughter is concerned: "Love bears all things, *believes all things*, hopes all things, endures all things" (1 Cor. 13:7). Ruby chose to believe her daughter.

But I'm skeptical. I seem to recall telling that same story to my mother when I was a teen. Perhaps Justine was indeed telling the truth, but our desire to believe the best about those we love shouldn't dull a healthy suspicion and a bit of deeper investigation. I hope my skepticism was ill-founded. I hope Justine wasn't lying. And I hope Ruby doesn't get her heart broken.

Watching over the ways of our household will always involve our work, our words, and our hearts.

as a businesswoman

Depending on your age, you might remember a television commercial that featured an attractive woman sashaying around her kitchen singing, "I can bring home the bacon, and fry it up in a pan and never, ever let you forget you're a man." I seem to recall it was a perfume commercial (go figure). In one sense, the woman in the commercial depicts something about the Proverbs 31 woman: she managed her domestic sphere while simultaneously working outside the home.

> She considers a field and buys it;
>> with the fruit of her hands she plants a vineyard.
>>> (Prov. 31:16)

> She makes linen garments and sells them;
>> she delivers sashes to the merchant. (Prov. 31:24)

This woman—one marked by wisdom—had the business know-how to purchase a field.

Christians typically come down strongly on one side or the other concerning whether it is biblical for wives, especially mothers, to work outside the home. We see from Proverbs that it is indeed biblical so long as it is applied within the framework of everything else Scripture teaches about wives and mothers.

In ancient Israel, women hiring themselves out as servants or even as slaves, while not common, was not unheard of. Throughout most of history, women have worked outside the home to help provide, most certainly in desperate times. That being said, we must balance that with what Paul wrote to Titus: "Older women likewise are to be reverent in behavior, not slanderers or slaves to much wine. They are to teach what is good, and so train the young women to love their husbands and children, to be self-controlled, pure, working at home, kind, and submissive to their own husbands, that the word of God may not be reviled" (Titus 2:3–5). Paul instructs that older women are to train younger women to focus their energies on their domestic responsibilities.

As we consider what we know about working women in ancient Israel, and what we see in the Proverbs 31 woman, alongside Paul's words here in Titus, we are able to come up with a biblical picture for application to our own lives. If we are being financially supported by our husband while raising children, yet we are considering going to work outside the home, Paul's words can serve as a siren to examine our motives. If we desire to go to work, we do well to ask ourselves these questions: (1) Am I seeking the good of others? (2) Will God be glorified more through what can be seen in my family? (3) Will my working benefit my family overall or just me? Let these questions guide your choice about whether going to work is wise.

These can be tricky questions for many of us. First, it is so easy in our society to confuse financial need with financial want. Elsewhere Paul wrote, "Godliness with contentment is great gain, for we brought nothing into the world, and we cannot take anything out of the world. But if we have food and clothing, with these we will be content" (1 Tim. 6:6–8). Paul wasn't saying we must go without that second car or pricey school. His point is about being satisfied with the basics. In other words, if we are considering going back to work so that we can fund some family fun in Europe this summer or a flat-screen TV, perhaps we need to reassess and realize that our kids would be better off finding us at home after school than they'd be with a few extras in the family toy chest.

Second, those questions can be tricky because of the external pressures we face. Society tells us that women are failures if they don't maximize their potential, or if they make sacrifices for the benefit of their families. To that end, let's be sure to note the context in which the Proverbs 31 woman exercised her business skills. She used them for the greater good of others, most especially for her family. Nowhere in this passage of Proverbs do we find anything about her going to work for the purpose of doing something "enriching," realizing her potential, or finding personal fulfillment.

We learn from the poem that exercising business skills while maintaining our unique call as nurturers of our family can certainly go hand in hand. It all depends on our reasons for putting those skills to use and how and where we choose to use them.

What about single women, who, by virtue of their singleness, must earn their living outside the home? Proverbs 31 principles apply just as much to them, because what we should glean from verses 16 and 24 isn't so much about working for a living as it is about maximizing our gifts, no matter our calling. Some time ago a single young woman wrote to a Christian blog and asked whether she should drop out of medical school. She hoped to meet a godly Christian man and get married someday, and she wondered if pursuing a medical degree would be detrimental to her marital hopes. The blogger did advise the young woman to quit the degree program, citing as her reason the fact that all the study was a waste of time and money, since the student hoped to be a stay-at-home wife and mother. This answer, I believe, lacked wisdom.

First, the young woman hoped to be married, but at the time of her question she had no particular young man even on her radar. Since she doesn't know the future—if or when she will get married—pursuing a medical education, if she has the aptitude and inclination to do so, seems like a good way to prepare to support herself if she doesn't marry or if she finds herself alone later in life. Second, if she does marry and winds up not practicing medicine as a career, she can certainly offer her medical skills and knowledge in service to her family, her church, and her community. Third, developing the gifts and talents God has given her is to exercise good stewardship of who God designed her to be, and it will conduce to his glory, whether or not those gifts wind up generating income.

If you are single and must earn a living or, at least, must prepare to do so, it is wise to take stock of your personal assets and cultivate them. It is not God-honoring to bury them for some potential future dream that may or may not come true. Some women don't allow themselves mental or educational development of any sort as they wait for Mr. Right. In some cases this is complementarianism run amok. In other cases, however unwitting, it is sometimes a sort of spiritual blackmail: "God *has* to give me a husband if I devote myself to nothing but preparing for that and that alone."

Lydia in the book of Acts was a successful businesswoman, and from what we know, a single woman, and her success did not compromise her femininity or her godliness. Maybe she'd had a husband at one point, or perhaps one came into her life later on. We don't know. We do know that she ran a successful business and was able to use the assets for the good of the baby church in Philippi. It is clear from Acts 16 that she had the sort of home into which she could host the apostles and provide for some of their needs.

Financial Know-How

Perhaps going to work is not an issue for you. Even so, there's still application to be made from the Proverbs 31 woman's head for business. She is portrayed as a woman in touch with the family financial picture. Can we say the same? We covered this in chapter 7, so we won't say much here except to consider once again, do we know what's in the savings account and the 401(k)? Are the bills up to date?

Even if we don't manage the money, maintaining a handle on the details is a good idea.

As I write, a woman I know comes to mind, Rachel. Her husband was killed in an accident last year, and her grief at the sudden loss was compounded by stress in the months that followed as notices of delinquent accounts piled up. Because her husband had always managed the money, she had no idea what was owed to whom and when it was due. Unraveling the tangle of bills and learning about insurance premiums and paying taxes overwhelmed Rachel, and today she recalls that issue as being one of the most difficult aspects of the tragedy. Do you know what your family financial situation is?

Wise women are also budget conscious. In other words, they live within their means. Something we can note about the woman in Proverbs is that being wise with money isn't just about frugality.

> She is not afraid of snow for her household,
> > for all her household are clothed in scarlet.
> She makes bed coverings for herself;
> > her clothing is fine linen and purple. (Prov. 31:21–22)

Fine linen, purple, and scarlet weren't inexpensive fabric choices. We learn from her that being budget conscious means knowing when to save a dollar and when a bit of extravagance is a good choice. Sometimes, as we consider the great needs in the world, we feel guilty about spending money on nice things, but we see something different here in Proverbs 31. Under ordinary circumstances, having nice things is one of the God-given benefits of wise living. That's what we are meant to see from this poem, as well as from the entire book of Proverbs. But if you read through the poem, you'll see that having nice things didn't come at the expense of other priorities. She was able to give to the poor *and* provide for her entire household.

So, whether in the home or out, single or married, there is a wisdom in being financially savvy.

a woman's wisdom

as a strong woman

Some months ago a popular women's magazine featured a photo of a well-dressed, perfectly coiffed woman posing as a body-builder and flexing her muscles. The caption underneath read, "Women can be strong, be smart, be sexy, be mothers, *and* be powerful. We don't need to compromise." That's not the sort of strength we see in the Proverbs 31 woman. She exudes strength, but hers is of a different sort altogether.

> She dresses herself with strength
> and makes her arms strong. (Prov. 31:17)

She does, however, keep herself physically fit, as we see from verse 17. There is wisdom in maintaining physical fitness—not the trendy sort that makes us feel backward if we aren't active participants in the local Pilates or Zumba class, but the sort that simply keeps us healthy. Many of us have bought into the myth that we must work out three times a week to realize any benefit, so because we don't have that kind of time to devote, we wind up doing nothing. For some reason, when it comes to exercise many of us have that all-or-nothing outlook. Yet a friend of mine keeps her triceps toned lifting soup cans, and another has done it by setting aside the mop and scrubbing her floors on hands and knees. If we are daunted by trendy forms of keeping fit, there are creative ways to work it into our daily routine.

In addition to strengthening her arms, the Proverbs 31 woman "dresses herself with strength." In other words, she covers herself with it. The wording here seems to indicate something more than physical prowess, and when we look at her life, we see that she is indeed dressed with mental and spiritual strength also, something she does by guarding her heart in the fear of the Lord. Verse 17 is said another way by the apostle Paul: "While bodily training is of some value, godliness is of value in every way, as it holds promise for the present life and also for the life to come" (1 Tim. 4:8).

as physically attractive

Busy as she is, she finds time to look nice.

> She makes bed coverings for herself;
>> her clothing is fine linen and purple. (Prov. 31:22)

Although this is the only mention of her appearance in the entire poem, even touching on this aspect of her person can turn some of us away from her altogether. After all, who has time to devote to outward appearance while caught up in the all-consuming tasks of raising children, managing our homes or careers, and serving in church? Something's got to give, and it seems that of all the competing priorities, this is the one. And for some women, personal appearance has always been a sore subject. However, it might seem a lot less intimidating if we consider it from the aspect of love rather than from the aspect of keeping up with the world.

Looking good by worldly standards has more to do with pride than with love. What besides pride could it be when the objective is to look as good as or better than our neighbors or colleagues? Surely that was not what the poet had in mind when he described the Proverbs 31 woman's attire. The fabrics she dons—fine linen and purple—were typically worn only by the prosperous, so we can assume the poet included these details to show the link between wisdom and prosperity. This point is reinforced by the fact that her entire family is clothed in costly scarlet (v. 21).

If we consider where else in the Bible we see scarlet and purple fabric, we wonder if the poet's symbolism goes even deeper. Certain items in the Old Testament tabernacle and temple were made of scarlet and purple yarns, as was the linen ephod and breastpiece worn by the priest (Exodus 26; 28; 35). There were also jewels in the breastpiece, and we find jewels in the Proverbs 31 poem too (v. 10). The color purple is associated with royalty and status, as we see in Esther 8:15. Purple is also linked to wealth, as we see positively in the Proverbs 31 poem and negatively in the parable of the rich man and Lazarus in Luke 16:19–31. Jesus was forcibly dressed in purple so that people could mock his claim to kingship (Mark 15:17, 20), although we know he was indeed a king—the King. On the other hand, in Revelation purple is a sign of the corrupting influences of money (17:4; 18:6).[3] The color scarlet in Scripture has both positive and negative associations, but we see it in a number of passages that have to do with purification (e.g., Lev. 14:4; Heb. 9:19–20).[4]

We certainly don't want to read into the poem meaning that isn't there, but at very least we can infer that the colors we find on the Proverbs 31 woman and in her home are meant to be symbolic of the nobility of wisdom.

In terms of practical considerations, we can simply say that she recognizes there is wisdom in presenting an attractive appearance. For one thing, her attractive appearance surely reflects well on her husband, and no doubt it pleases him. And if we think back to the advice given to husbands earlier in Proverbs, we see that her efforts to look nice will aid him in following it:

> Let your fountain be blessed,
>   and rejoice in the wife of your youth,
>   a lovely deer, a graceful doe.
> Let her breasts fill you at all times with delight;
>   be intoxicated always in her love.
> Why should you be intoxicated, my son, with a forbidden
>   woman
>   and embrace the bosom of an adulteress? (Prov.
>   5:18–20)

From her we learn that making some effort to look attractive is a way to love our husbands. It's also a way to love God. He is not glorified by women who let themselves go. That being said, it's not an attractive appearance that brings him glory so much as it is the careful stewardship of her person that her appearance indicates.

Rachel Held Evans writes, "I've found nothing in the Bible to suggest that God requires women to be beautiful. . . . While young love is certainly celebrated in the Bible (Song of Songs, Proverbs 5:15–19), there is nothing to suggest that a woman is expected to maintain a certain standard of beauty throughout all phases of life in order to adequately please her husband."[5] Evans is right in at least one regard: there is nothing in the Bible that mandates a woman maintain her looks. However, as we learn from the Proverbs 31 woman, there is most definitely wisdom in doing so. Evans wrote her article to address the remarks made by some leading evangelicals who urge women to look good so that their husbands won't stray. It is indeed regrettable if leaders place blame for cheating husbands on a wife's failure to maintain her appearance; the blame for a husband's unfaithfulness can never rightly be placed there. However, a woman can certainly help her husband avoid temptation by making a bit of effort with her appearance, and in this way, it can rightly be viewed as an act of love, not desperation. If any woman fears that she must look good to keep her man faithful, the problem, it seems to me, has more to do with the health of the marriage than with anything about the woman's looks.

Looking nice is a way to love our husband, but there is a huge difference between making effort and obsessing. There is no wisdom in a preoccupation with looks, as the poem makes clear:

> Charm is deceitful, and beauty is vain,
>> but a woman who fears the LORD is to be praised.
>> (Prov. 31:30)

The point of the verse isn't that looks count for nothing; it's that looks, when weighed in the balance with godliness and all other aspects of wisdom, count for very little. As we view verse 30 in light of the whole poem, we can determine where to put physical appearance on our priority list (low) and what motive should govern those efforts (love). In other words, making a well-balanced effort with our appearance while also recognizing its limited value is one aspect of a woman's wisdom. We see beautiful women on television or around town and note their beauty, but we forget them as soon as they pass on by. Conversely, we tend to remember women who make substantive contributions to the world, no matter what they look like, and we can note that the women most respected in the world are not the most beautiful.

as confident

If we had to pick a single word to describe the Proverbs 31 woman, a good choice would be *confident*.

> She is not afraid of snow for her household,
> > for all her household are clothed in scarlet. (Prov. 31:21)

> Strength and dignity are her clothing,
> > and she laughs at the time to come. (Prov. 31:25)

First, she is confident because her family is well provided for (v. 21). She isn't worried about having sufficient resources to feed and clothe those who live in her domain. We might be quick to say, "Well, it would be easy not to fear if I had lots of money like she had," but if we land there, we miss the point, which is that wisdom is what led to the financial provision in the first place. What we see here again is an example of the principle shown throughout the book of Proverbs that wise living typically leads to the sort of blessings that prevent many of the things we often worry about.

Second, she is confident because she has a good reputation. She is known for her strength and dignity (v. 25). We see throughout the poem how her reputation blesses her. It has opened doors for business and for ministry, and it has brought her the praise of her husband and children:

> Her children rise up and call her blessed;
> > her husband also, and he praises her:
> "Many women have done excellently,
> > but you surpass them all." (Prov. 31:28–29)

The same is true in our lives. Our reputation steers our course in ways big and small. Our financial reputation, for example, is reflected in our credit score, and the better our credit score, the more options we have when it comes to making purchases or investing. Just so, our reputation for trustworthiness will largely determine the number and quality of our relationships. Our reputation for diligence opens doors in education and in business. A reputation for godliness attracts those who seek the Lord, whether for ministry, friendship, or marriage. A life lived in the fear of the Lord imparts a reputation for wisdom, and it glorifies God.

Third, she is confident because she is not afraid of what the future might hold (v. 25). She doesn't fret over a possible downturn in the economy, or whether her children will be successful, or whether she'll remain healthy as she ages. She certainly does not know what the future holds—no amount of wisdom reveals that to her or to anyone. The economy might go sour, and her kids might choose foolish paths despite the wisdom imparted by their parents, and she might be stricken with serious illness. So how can she laugh at the time to come? She is unafraid because she trusts in the Lord. We know this because she is presented as the ideal of wisdom in a book that teaches that the heart of wisdom is the fear of the Lord. Ultimately, her fear of the Lord, not her material prosperity, is why she is confident.

So, as we consider our battles with anxiety from the perspective of Proverbs, is it possible that our battles are rooted in the fact that either we are choosing to live unwisely somehow or we aren't trusting God? Actually, the two go together. We aren't going to choose paths of wisdom if we don't trust the One who has marked out those paths for us. Fear of the Lord is trust in the Lord.

a woman's wisdom

Primarily, the Proverbs 31 woman is confident because she fears the Lord. This is the bedrock of all her wise behaviors. She is a good wife and mother, and industrious, and financially shrewd, and kind, and well-spoken, and charitable because her entire being is oriented around the fear of the Lord. That is the only way for us too. "The fear of the LORD is the beginning of wisdom" (Prov. 9:10). Even so, we will never get there on our own. We cannot get established in the fear of the Lord or grow wise apart from Christ our Savior. Elyse Fitzpatrick warns:

> The plain words of the proverbs are for our good, and we will grow in wisdom if we respond to them in faith and humility. It is just that if we neglect to see Jesus there too, we will wrongly assume that we will be able to automatically accomplish something that not even Solomon could accomplish: producing wise children. In addition, because the proverbs are so clear-cut and seem like promises, we'll believe that our performance will guarantee success. Many so-called Christian parenting books develop the parental wisdom in Proverbs without any recognition of the presence of the Christ.[6]

That's why growing in wisdom means looking more at Christ than at the Proverbs 31 woman. We cannot be like her by ourselves. We can only do it in dependence on Christ, because he *is* our wisdom. Elyse points out beautifully how this is so:

> If we approach the proverbs believing that the entire Bible "whispers his name," if we come with open eyes, looking for our Savior, we'll easily identify him there as the Wise Son. Yes, the proverbs do tell us how to live godly lives, but they also tell us about him. For instance, the command, "My son, if sinners entice you, do not consent," was abundantly fulfilled in Jesus's resistance to Satan's temptations in the wilderness. Jesus is the Wise Son who always did what was pleasing to his Father (Isa. 52:13; John 8:29). And although the Bible is nearly silent on Jesus's childhood, we do have this one description: "Jesus increased in wisdom and in

stature and in favor with God and man" (Luke 2:52). He was completely obedient because he was fully wise, and he was loved by his Father and his parents. Jesus even refers to himself as the personification of wisdom (Matt. 11:19), while Paul assures us that in him are hidden *all* the treasures of wisdom and knowledge (Col. 2:3). Jesus is the denouement of Proverbs' Wise Son.[7]

her rewards

What does the Proverbs 31 woman receive as a result of her wisdom? We'll wrap up our study with a list of ten rewards:

1) She is valued (v. 10)
2) She has a solid marriage (vv. 11, 12, 28)
3) She lives without fear (vv. 21, 25)
4) She is materially comfortable (vv. 21, 22)
5) She is tangibly successful (vv. 16, 18, 24)
6) She is not easily wearied (vv. 15, 17, 18, 27)
7) She has a good reputation (vv. 25, 29)
8) She is praised by her family (vv. 28–29)
9) She has a heart that overflows with active love (vv. 20, 26)
10) She knows the Lord (v. 30)

She is the picture of wise living, but not primarily of how to be a better homemaker or businesswoman. The picture she provides is how full and rewarding a woman's life can be if she fears the Lord.

> Give her of the fruit of her hands,
>   and let her works praise her in the gates. (Prov. 31:31)

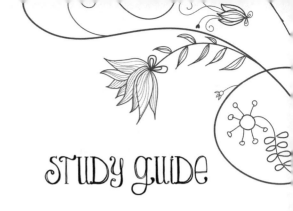

STUDY GUIDE

Note to reader: This guide can be printed out at a larger size at crossway.org/awomanswisdom.

You can work through this study guide on your own or as part of a small-group discussion. There is at least one question in each chapter that will require a bit more time than the other questions. These questions are marked with a special symbol: 🌿 You might also want to use the appendix as a handy way of reviewing various proverbs.

chapter one
what, exactly, is wisdom?

🌿 1. Read through the book of Esther and jot down where and how you see her exercising wisdom. What impact do her choices have on her relative Mordecai? What sort of impact does she have on the king?

2. Name an area of your life (or more than one) in which you desire to grow in wisdom. Why do you think you need wisdom in this particular area?

3. How does Proverbs define wisdom? Explain what is meant by this definition.

4. Have you ever experienced fear of God? What did you learn about him through that time? What was the outcome?

5. Which of the characteristics of wisdom listed in chapter 1 most speak to you and why?

- Wisdom is clear

- Wisdom is near

- Wisdom is pleasant

- Wisdom is primary

- Wisdom is hospitable

6. Describe what it means to guard your heart (Prov. 4:23).

7. What is the link between wisdom and humility, and how do we cultivate humility?

8. What is our role in obtaining wisdom?

9. Which of the benefits of wisdom grabs you most and why?

- Security

- Guidance

- Sanctified common sense

- Generally good living

- Happiness

- Self-knowledge

10. Describe the biblical link between Christ and wisdom.

chapter two
why folly is really bad

1. What is the primary distinction between a foolish woman and a wise one? *God*

2. Name some ways that women today can be easily enticed by the world. What for you personally tends to be an enticement? *Books   discontentment*

🌿 3. There are many proverbs that mention money or wealth (see the appendix). Why do you think that this Bible book about wisdom has this emphasis? We also find a number of passages about wealth in the New Testament that address it primarily in terms of its impact on Christian discipleship. Study the following passages and summarize what you see:

- Matthew 6:25–34

  God Provides

- Matthew 13:18–23

- Luke 16:13

- Acts 8:9–21

- 1 Timothy 3:2–3

- 1 Timothy 6:6–10, 17–19

- 2 Timothy 3:1–5

- Hebrews 13:5–6

- James 5:1–6

4. In what ways does a foolish woman show contempt for godly knowledge?

Pride

5. How can we tell the difference between patient waiting and sinful complacency? As you ponder the difference, does it speak to your life in some way? *worring or planning*

6. Where in your life do you detect a need to become more like the ant of Proverbs 6:6–8? Is there a lack of zeal in your work, in your relationships, or in your walk of faith? If so, what concrete step will you take to address it? *read every day this week*

7. In a society that upholds autonomy as a great virtue, living in dependence on God and in transparency before your Christian community can be especially challenging. Describe the difference between godly independence and sinful autonomy. Consider Proverbs 18:1 and 1 Thessalonians 4:9–12.

8. Review Proverbs 6:16–19. From this passage make a list of things God hates so much that they are categorized as "abominations." Then, using this list, pray the prayer found in Psalm 139:23–24 either alone or with your small group:

> Search me, O God, and know my heart!
> Try me and know my thoughts!
> And see if there be any grievous way in me,
> and lead me in the way everlasting!

You also might want to see if you find yourself resonating with something on the why-oh-why and if-only list on pp 51–52.

9. In what way is overcoming our folly more a matter of rest than of work?

10. How do the following passages showcase Jesus as our wisdom?

- Matthew 12:38–42

- Luke 2:40–52

- 1 Corinthians 1:18–31

- 1 Corinthians 2:1–13

- Colossians 2:1–3

- Colossians 2:20–23

- Colossians 3:16

chapter three

wise women know the power of words

1. What important part do our words play in our role as helpers? Keeping in mind the examples we considered from Scripture (Esther and Delilah), describe a time when your words swayed a situation for good or ill. Is there a particular teaching from Proverbs that your experience proved true?

2. Proverbs offers a good bit of insight into the destructive nature of lying. Where have you seen those truths worked out in your own life? (You might want to review specific proverbs using the appendix).

3. In what ways is the term *false witness* much broader than just telling the truth in court?

4. Of the particular speech follies we covered in chapter 3, are there any that you have always viewed as no big deal? If so, how has your view about them changed as a result of studying Proverbs?

5. Some types of talk, while not outright sinful, are nevertheless foolish. What, according to Proverbs, is included in this category?

6. Is gossip a struggle for you, whether with tongue or ear? What truths from Proverbs about gossip most directly impact you and why? Select one proverb about gossip to memorize.

7. Is there something in your life at present that might make you susceptible to flattery? How will you guard against it specifically?

8. What are some characteristics of wise words?

9. How are our ears linked to our tongues when it comes to wisdom?

❧ 10. Read the following verses about wise and foolish talk from James, the New Testament book of wisdom. What do you find here that reinforces or builds on what you learned from Proverbs?

- James 1:19–20

- James 1:26

- James 2:8–12

- James 2:14–17

- James 3:2–12

- James 4:11–12

- James 4:13–16

- James 5:12

chapter four

wise women choose friends carefully

1. With whom do you spend the most time? How did these friendships come about and develop?

Judy - mentor   Christina M. - High Sch.
Terri - College   Eva - homeschool

2. What tends to draw you to particular friendships? Consider both the pitfalls and the godly qualities we looked at in chapter 4.

Brooke C - Needed me   Terri + July - stability,
Eva - uniqueness

3. Are any of your friendships characterized by chaos? If so, what proverbs address that, and how?

LisaAnn Prov 13:20

❧ 4. Proverbs cautions us against giving our hearts to angry people. Why? Consider developing a fuller biblical picture of anger by studying the following passages:

God's Anger	Man's (Woman's) Anger
Ex. 32:1–10 *Is did not obey*	Gen. 4:1–7 *doing the min wanting Max*
Num. 11:1 *quick and direct*	2 Sam. 6:5–10 *not trusting*
2 Sam. 6:5–10 *Smote individual*	Ps. 4:4 *BOK*
1 Kings 11:1–9 *turned from God*	Ps. 37:8 *anger → Devil*
2 Chron. 28:22–25 *Live in Evil*	Eccles. 7:9 *foolish*
Ps. 30:5 *endureth a moment*	Jonah 4:1–9 *selfish*
Ps. 38:1–4 *for correction*	Matt. 5:22 *often baseless*
Ps. 85:1–8 *turns to salvation*	John 7:32–33 *murmuring*

God's Anger	Man's (Woman's) Anger
Ps. 86:15 *longsuffering*	2 Cor. 12:20 *leads to bad behavior*
Ps. 90:1–12 *planned*	Gal. 5:20 *leads to bad character*
Isa. 57:16–17	Eph. 4:26
Jer. 3:6–13	Eph. 4:31
Jer. 4:22–26	Eph. 6:4
Hos. 14:1–4	Col. 3:8
Mark 3:1–6	James 1:19–20

5. Why must we be cautious in deepening a bond with someone given to sensual indulgence? What sorts of indulgences might this include beyond just food and drink?

6. What are some of the biblical principles for choosing wisely in friendships? In keeping with that, do you have an "iron" friend (Prov. 27:17)? What about that relationship causes mutual sharpening?

7. Do you find it difficult to speak up when you see your friend straying from godly paths? What is the perceived risk you fear? What is the

difference between speaking truth in love and judgmental criticism? How do you think we can distinguish between the two?

8. Have you ever been caught in an idolatrous relationship? If so, what bad fruits of idolatry were evidenced? How did the relationship end? If it hasn't yet ended, describe how the steps of repentance in Hosea 14 can help you.

9. What does Scripture say about friendships with professing believers who live in unrepentant sin? How do we determine when to move closer to the sinning one and when to move away?

10. Jesus, of course, is the ultimate friend. What do these verses teach about this aspect of our relationship with him:

- Exodus 33:9–11

- Psalm 25:14

- Luke 7:33–35

- John 15:13–15

- James 4:4

chapter five

wise women know the secret of self-control

1. In what area do you find self-control to be a perpetual struggle?

anger

2. What is gluttony? Why can those who eat too little be considered gluttons?

❧ 3. How can we eat to the glory of God? Use the following passages to provide an answer.

- Psalm 104:14–15

- Psalm 104:24–26

- Proverbs 23:20–21

- Proverbs 25:16, 27

- Proverbs 27:7

- Matthew 6:25–33

- Romans 14:13–21

- 1 Corinthians 8:8–13

• 1 Corinthians 10:23–33

• 2 Thessalonians 3:10–12

• 1 Timothy 6:17

4. How does Proverbs 25:28 describe self-control? From where does the analogy of broken-down walls come, and why is it a fitting analogy?

5. Read Romans 1:18–32. Describe the downward spiral of sin. Based on this passage, what causes someone to get stuck in a destructive sin pattern, in what today is called "addiction"? How does Galatians 5:17–26 show us the way out?

6. Which of the five hindrances that we considered in chapter 5 might best describe your personal struggle with self-control?

7. How does James 4:2–3 factor into the struggle with self-control?

8. How do Colossians 1:29 and Philippians 2:12–13 speak to our efforts at self-control?

study guide

❧ 9. What place does alcohol hold in your convictions? Does that differ from what you practice? Meditate on the following passages and those in the appendix that mention the consumption of alcohol:

- Numbers 6:1–21

- Psalm 104:14–15

- Luke 2:1–12

- Romans 13:10–14

- Romans 14:13–23

- Ephesians 5:15–21

- 1 Thessalonians 5:5–8

- 1 Timothy 3:8

- Titus 2:1–4

- 1 Peter 4:1–3

10. Ultimately, what four factors lead to self-control?

chapter six

wise women know how to think, feel, and want

1. Discuss or describe the ways in which our thoughts, feelings, and desires can shape our lives. Provide some concrete examples.

2. Why is it wise to give greater weight to thoughts than to feelings?

3. What is the link between humility and wise thinking?

4. Read the following passages about thoughts:

   • Romans 8:5–7; 12:1–2

   • 2 Corinthians 10:4–6

   • Ephesians 4:17–24

   • Philippians 2:3–8

study guide

- Colossians 3:1–3

- 1 Peter 1:10–16

What imperatives (commands) do you see that pertain to our thought life? Why, according to these verses, is our thought life so vital to our faith?

5. Contrast single-mindedness and double-mindedness. You might first want to read Psalm 119:113 and James 1:5–8; 4:1–8.

6. Discuss or describe what it means to be obsessed with something or someone. How can obsessions impact us spiritually? Why is it wise to guard ourselves against obsessive thoughts?

7. Review what Proverbs teaches about anger (see, e.g., Prov. 10:11; 14:29; 15:18; 16:32). What can we learn about anger from the life of Jesus? Ephesians 4:26 warns us, "Be angry and do not sin; do not let the sun go down on your anger." What are some ways we can handle anger without sin?

❧ 8. In what way was David's grief excessive? (Read 2 Sam. 18:1–19:8.) How can we handle grief with godliness?

9. What turns a good desire into a sinful one? What does Proverbs teach about desires that are aligned with God's truth? (See Prov. 10:24; 11:23.)

10. According to Proverbs, how can we handle our desires in a godly manner?

chapter seven

wise women are financially savvy

1. Do you have an informed understanding of your personal or familial financial picture? Why or why not?

2. In what way can keeping abreast of family finances be a way in which we fulfill our calling as helper in marriage?

3. Discuss or describe the overall teaching of Proverbs about money management. To what does Proverbs link financial prosperity?

4. What does Proverbs teach about borrowing money? How do you think this teaching can be applied wisely in our present-day culture?

5. Proverbs 22:7 says, "The rich rules over the poor, and the borrower is the slave of the lender." Discuss or describe how you've seen this played out in your life or in the life of someone you know.

6. Discuss or describe some of the stresses that can accompany wealth.

❧ 7. Read the following passages that mention money:

- Proverbs 3:9; 13:11

- Ecclesiastes 5:10–12

- Matthew 6:24–33

- 1 Timothy 6:6–10

- Hebrews 13:5–6

Describe the attitude that a disciple of Jesus should have toward money. How does your attitude align with Scripture's teaching?

8. Reread the prayer of Agur in Proverbs 30:8–9. Can you wholeheartedly make Agur's prayer your own? If not, why not?

9. Why can money be a spiritual danger?

10. Discuss or describe from Scripture why there is hope for Christians who are floundering due to unwise financial decisions.

chapter eight

wise women safeguard their sexuality

1. What was the original purpose for Proverbs' instructions about sexual purity? Why is this instruction important for today's women?

2. Discuss or describe why sexual activity outside of marriage is evil. Base your answer on Scripture passages such as 1 Corinthians 3:1–13; 6:12–20; and 1 Thessalonians 4:3–8.

3. Why are we so susceptible to sexual temptation?

4. Identify the consequences for sexual sin put forth in Proverbs 5:9–21 and 7:22–27. Where have you observed the reality of these consequences?

5. What link do we find in Proverbs between immoral behavior and discontentment?

6. Discuss or describe some character traits of the immoral woman in Proverbs.

7. Discuss or describe some practical ways to avoid sexual sin.

8. Why is adultery a direct attack on marriage and not merely a violation of it?

9. What are some ways Proverbs gives for safeguarding our marriage from adultery? How might these safeguards be applied practically in our own marriage?

❧ 10. Read the story of David and Bathsheba in 2 Samuel 11:1–12:23. What truths from Proverbs about adultery do you see manifested in this story?

chapter nine
the woman of proverbs 31

1. How does the Proverbs 31 woman function in the book of Proverbs—in other words, how are we meant to view her?

2. In what ways does the Proverbs 31 woman depict a wife who can be trusted?

3. Considered in light of how the statement was discussed in chapter 9, do you agree that all women are called to be homemakers? Why or why not?

4. The Proverbs 31 woman is depicted as active from before sunrise till long after sundown. We aren't meant to make a literal application of that to our lives—we couldn't anyway! But what changes can we make to our lives to better fulfill Paul's mandate in Ephesians 5:15–16, "Look carefully then how you walk, not as unwise but as wise, making the best use of the time, because the days are evil"?

❧ 5. Read the stories of the wives in Scripture (listed below). Give concrete examples of how they compare and contrast with the ideal wife of Proverbs 31.

- Rebekah (Gen. 25:19–27; 27:1–35)

- Abigail (1 Sam. 25:1–42)

- Michal (2 Sam. 6:16–23)

- Jezebel (1 Kings 21:1–16)

- Sapphira (Acts 5:1–10)

- Priscilla (Acts 18:1–27)

6. Discuss or describe all the ways the Proverbs 31 woman is held forth as a nurturer.

7. What is your view of mothers working outside the home? Does the Proverbs 31 woman influence your view? What do we see in the poem that made her business endeavors godly rather than sinfully selfish?

8. What can we learn from the Proverbs 31 woman about the value of a woman's personal appearance? What makes an effort to look attractive either godly or worldly?

9. What is the significance of the fabrics we find in the poem?

10. The Proverbs 31 woman is depicted as confident (vv. 21, 25). What is the basis for her confidence?

appendix

some topics in proverbs

appendix

Some good books for wise women

Boice, James Montgomery. *Romans*, 4 vols. Grand Rapids, MI: Baker, 1995.

Bridges, Jerry. *The Discipline of Grace: God's Role and Our Role in the Pursuit of Holiness*. New ed. Colorado Springs, CO: NavPress, 2006.

———. *The Gospel for Real Life: Turn to the Liberating Power of the Cross . . . Every Day*. Colorado Springs, CO: NavPress, 2003.

———. *Trusting God: Even When Life Hurts*. Colorado Springs, CO: NavPress, 1989.

Burroughs, Jeremiah. *The Rare Jewel of Christian Contentment*. Carlisle, PA: Banner of Truth, 1964.

Challies, Tim. *The Discipline of Spiritual Discernment*. Wheaton, IL: Crossway, 2007.

Chapell, Bryan. *Holiness by Grace: Delighting in the Joy That Is Our Strength*. Wheaton, IL: Crossway, 2003.

DeMoss, Nancy Leigh. *Brokenness, Surrender, Holiness: A Revive Our Hearts Trilogy*. Chicago: Moody, 2008.

Elliot, Elisabeth. *Discipline: The Glad Surrender*. Grand Rapids, MI: Revell, 1985.

Ferguson, Sinclair. *Discovering God's Will*. Carlisle, PA: Banner of Truth, 1982.

Fitzpatrick, Elyse. *Because He Loves Me: How God Transforms Our Daily Life*. Wheaton, IL: Crossway, 2010.

———. *Idols of the Heart: Learning to Long for God Alone*. Phillipsburg, NJ: P&R, 2002.

———. *Love to Eat, Hate to Eat: Breaking the Bondage of Destructive Eating Habits*. Eugene, OR: Harvest, 2004.

Fitzpatrick, Elyse, and Carol Cornish, eds. *Women Helping Women: A Biblical Guide to Major Issues Women Face*. Eugene, OR: Harvest, 1997.

Guinness, Os. *The Call: Finding and Fulfilling the Central Purpose of Your Life*. Nashville: Nelson, 2003.

Guthrie, Nancy. *The Wisdom of God: Seeing Jesus in the Psalms and Wisdom Books*. Wheaton, IL: Crossway, 2012.

Horton, Michael. *Christless Christianity: The Alternative Gospel of the American Church*. Grand Rapids, MI: Baker, 2008.

Hughes, Barbara. *Disciplines of a Godly Woman*. Wheaton, IL: Crossway, 2006.

Lane, Timothy S., and Paul David Tripp. *How People Change*. Greensboro, NC: New Growth Press, 2008.

Lloyd-Jones, Martyn. *Spiritual Depression: Its Causes and Cure*. Grand Rapids, MI: Eerdmans, 1965.

Lundgaard, Kris. *The Enemy Within: Straight Talk about the Power and Defeat of Sin*. Phillipsburg, NJ: P&R, 1998.

Mack, Wayne A. *Humility: The Forgotten Virtue*. Phillipsburg, NJ: P&R, 2005.

Matzat, Don. *Christ Esteem: Where the Search for Self-Esteem Ends*. Eugene, OR: Harvest, 1990.

Moore, Russell. *Tempted and Tried: Temptation and the Triumph of Christ*. Wheaton, IL: Crossway, 2011.

Nielson, Kathleen, *Proverbs: The Ways of Wisdom*. Phillipsburg, NJ: P&R.

Packer, J. I. *God's Plan for You*. Wheaton, IL: Crossway, 2001.

———. *Knowing God*. Downers Grove, IL: InterVarsity, 1977.

Pink, A. W. *Practical Christianity*. Grand Rapids, MI: Baker, 1978.

Piper, John. *Don't Waste Your Life*. Wheaton, IL: Crossway, 2007.

Smart, Dominic. *When We Get It Wrong: Peter, Christ and Our Path Through Failure*. Authentic Publishing, 2005.

Welch, Edward T. *When People Are Big and God Is Small: Overcoming Peer Pressure, Codependency, and the Fear of Man*. Phillipsburg, NJ: P&R, 1997.

NOTES

Chapter 1: What, Exactly, Is Wisdom?

1. William Harrell, "The Fear of the Lord," http://www.banneroftruth.org/pages/articles/article_detail.php?66.
2. My former pastor James Montgomery Boice recounted this story in his own writings, which is where I learned of it.
3. One of the best books to read on all Jesus has already done for us is Dominic Smart, *When We Get It Wrong: Peter, Christ and Our Path Through Failure* (Authentic, 2005).

Chapter 2: Why Folly Is Really Bad

1. J. C. Ryle, *Holiness* (Darlington, UK: Evangelical Press, 1999), 46.

Chapter 3: Wise Women Know the Power of Words

1. Westminster Larger Catechism Q. 144.
2. D. A. Carson, *Jesus' Sermon on the Mount and His Confrontation with the World: An Exposition of Matthew 5–10* (Grand Rapids, MI: Global Christian, 1999), 113.

Chapter 4: Wise Women Choose Friends Carefully

1. Edward Welch, *When People Are Big and God Is Small: Overcoming Peer Pressure, Codependency, and the Fear of Man* (Phillipsburg, NJ: P&R, 1997), 13–14; emphasis original.
2. James Montgomery Boice, *Minor Prophets: Two Volumes Complete in One Edition* (Grand Rapids, MI: Kregel, 1986), 94.

Chapter 5: Wise Women Know the Secret of Self-Control

1. http://www.bravotv.com/top-chef/season-8/blogs/gail-simmons/pepperoni-sauce?page=0,1.
2. James Montgomery Boice, *Romans, An Expositional Commentary, vol. 1: Justification by Faith* (Grand Rapids, MI: Baker, 1991), 199–200.
3. John Piper, "Total Abstinence and Church Membership," http://www.desiringgod.org/resource-library/sermons/total-abstinence-and-church-membership.

notes

4. Don Matzat, *Christ Esteem: Where the Search for Self-Esteem Ends* (Eugene, OR: Harvest House, 1990), 109; emphasis original.

Chapter 6: Wise Women Know How to Think, Feel, and Want

1. Michael R. Emlet, "Obsession and Compulsions: Breaking Free of the Tyranny," *Journal of Biblical Counseling*, vol. 22 (Winter 2004): 16, 23–24.
2. James Montgomery Boice, *Philippians*, An Expositional Commentary (Grand Rapids, MI: Baker n.d.), 248–49.
3. James Montgomery Boice, *Romans*, vol 4: *The New Humanity*, An Expositional Commentary (Grand Rapids, MI: Baker, 1995), 1558–59.
4. Elisabeth Elliot, *Discipline: The Glad Surrender* (Grand Rapids, MI: Revell, 1982), 151.
5. Bryan Chapell, *Ephesians*, Reformed Expository Commentary (Phillipsburg, NJ: 2009), 222.
6. Arthur W. Pink, *The Life of David* (Grand Rapids, MI: Baker, 1981), 190. His extensive treatment of David's grief makes for insightful reading.
7. David Powlison, "Dynamics of Biblical Change," CCEF course materials, 1995.

Chapter 7: Wise Women Are Financially Savvy

1. J. I. Packer, *Knowing God* (Downers Grove, IL: InterVarsity, 1973), 227–28.

Chapter 8: Wise Women Safeguard Their Sexuality

1. Katrina Trinko, "On the Books: Excerpts from State Adultery Laws," http://www.usatoday.com/news/opinion/forum/2010-04-26-column26_ST_N.htm.
2. Jonathan Turley, "Adultery in Many States Is Still a Crime," *USA Today*, April 25, 2010, http://www.usatoday.com/news/opinion/forum/2010-04-26-column26_ST_N.htm.
3. Derek Kidner, *Proverbs: An Introduction and Commentary* (Leicester: Inter-Varsity, 1964), 69; emphasis original.
4. Ibid., 71.
5. James Montgomery Boice, *The Minor Prophets: Two Volumes Complete in One Edition* (Grand Rapids, MI: Kregel, 1996), 116–17.

Chapter 9: The Woman of Proverbs 31

1. Douglas Sean O'Donnell, *The Beginning and End of Wisdom: Preaching Christ from the First and Last Chapters of Proverbs, Ecclesiastes, and Job* (Wheaton, IL: Crossway, 2011), 50–51.
2. John Piper, *Don't Waste Your Life* (Wheaton, IL: Crossway, 2007), 120.
3. For more information, see http://www.biblebasics.co.uk/colours/col12.htm.
4. See http://www.biblebasics.co.uk/colours/col8.htm.
5. http://rachelheldevans.com/thou-shalt-not-let-thyself-go-mark-driscoll-haggard.
6. Elyse Fitzpatrick and Jessica Thompson, *Give them Grace: Dazzling your Kids with the Love of Jesus* (Wheaton, IL: Crossway, 2011), 99–100.
7. Ibid., 99.

General Index

general index

SCRIPTURE INDEX

Take Your Study to Greater Depth with the Teaching DVD

Featuring Lydia Brownback

a woman's WISDOM

how the book of Proverbs

DVD

lydia brownback

Coming in Fall 2012

This new DVD companion to the book features nine teaching sessions showing women how the wisdom of Proverbs is meant to govern real-life issues such as relationships, sexuality, emotions, and the words we speak. Perfect for small group and individual study.